To Ken,
Just a little something t[illegible]
of the past.
With Love
George [illegible]arol.
Christmas 1984.

Gareth Edwards' Most
Memorable Matches

# Gareth Edwards' Most Memorable Matches

with Terry Godwin

*Cartoons by Roy Ullyett*

Stanley Paul
London Melbourne Sydney Auckland Johannesburg

Stanley Paul & Co. Ltd

An imprint of the Hutchinson Publishing Group

17–21 Conway Street, London W1P 6JD

Hutchinson Publishing Group (Australia) Pty Ltd
PO Box 496, 16–22 Church Street, Hawthorne, Melbourne, Victoria 3122

Hutchinson Group (NZ) Ltd
32–34 View Road, PO Box 40–086, Glenfield, Auckland 10

Hutchinson Group (SA) Pty Ltd
PO Box 337, Bergvlei 2012, South Africa

First published 1984


Set in Linotron Baskerville by Input Typesetting Ltd, London

Printed and bound in Great Britain by Anchor Brendon Ltd,
Tiptree, Essex

British Library Cataloguing in Publications Data

Edwards, Gareth
Gareth Edwards' most memorable matches.
1. Edwards, Gareth 2. Rugby Football
players—Wales—Biography
I. Title
796.33'3'0924 GV944.9.E38

ISBN 0 09 153590 5

# Contents

# Acknowledgement

I would like to thank Terry Godwin for his invaluable assistance in writing this book.

# Photo Acknowledgement

The publishers would like to thank Colin Elsey of Colorsport for providing the copyright photographs in this book.

# 1 Wales *versus* England

As every Welsh rugby fan knows, no match is more important than the one against England. Regardless of whether a Triple Crown or a Grand Slam is at stake, or whether the match is at the Arms Park or Twickenham, the confrontation with the Old Enemy is always special, something to savour, and greeted with eager anticipation by player and supporter alike. As Bill Shankly was fond of saying, it's not just a matter of life and death, it's more important than that.

A win against France, the Scots or the Irish is always welcome. But there is nothing the Welsh supporter relishes more than a victory over the English – especially if it is achieved at Twickenham. On the other hand, defeat by England is mortifying for a Welshman. Nothing is more calculated to send him into the deepest of depressions.

I count myself fortunate to have played against England in an era when defeats were rare. I played against them twelve times and I like to think I helped redress the balance of the 'bad old days' before 1949, when Wales were usually on the losing end against England. In fact, the only time I played in a losing side against England was in 1974, which was Wales's only defeat against them in sixteen matches between 1964 and 1979. That was a sad day, I recall, for two of Wales's greatest forwards, Dai Morris and Delme Thomas. Neither was invited to wear a Welsh jersey again after we had gone down 12–16 at Twickenham, courtesy of some astute tactical play by England's fly half, Alan Old.

The three matches I remember best against England were those in 1967, 1969 and 1978. And the most memorable of these was the middle one, at the Arms Park in 1969 when, after good wins over Scotland and Ireland, Wales were seeking the Triple Crown. What a day it was. What a match!

That side of '69 not only won the Triple Crown, but formed, I believe, the basis, in terms of players, attitude and strategy, of the all-conquering Welsh sides of the seventies. The 1967 match was my first against England; the 1978 one coincided with my fiftieth international appearance. But that 1969 match was just that little bit more special, not only for me, but for two of Wales's greatest points scorers, Keith Jarrett and Maurice Richards.

## Wales 34 England 21, Cardiff Arms Park, 15 April 1967

My first appearance in a Welsh jersey at Cardiff Arms Park coincided with Wales's biggest score ever against England and England's biggest points haul ever in Wales. The spectacular, history-making scoring in the match, however, was a footnote to an occasion when the headlines evocatively heralded the arrival of yet another in the unending list of Welsh rugby heroes. As long as England and Wales continue to wage their annual battle, this will always be known as Keith Jarrett's match.

Even today, people are incredulous and awed by Jarrett's debut. Although physically well made, the 6-foot, 13-stone Jarrett was in all respects a fresh-faced schoolboy. At eighteen, he had left Monmouth School only four months previously and had had only sixteen first-class matches in the centre for Newport. With Terry Price seemingly a fixture at fullback for Wales – until his position became suspect after a poor match against France – not even the most audacious speculators would have suggested the fledgling, for all his burgeoning talent, would be selected to take Price's place. But, in keeping with the time-honoured eccentricity of Welsh selection, the youngster received his call-up when Price was dropped, never to play for Wales again. Clearly Jarrett's phenomenal kicking ability – he had scored over 100 points since joining Newport – fanned selectorial interest. But the selectors wanted him at fullback not centre, since Gerald Davies and Billy Raybould constructively occupied the midfield. Consequently Newport were requested to give the precocious Jarrett some experience of the fullback position by playing him there against Newbridge, but the match was such a disaster that Jarrett reverted to his customary centre position in the second half. Despite this, and largely because of his kicking potential, Jarrett was picked. It was a gamble which paid off handsomely.

In truth, I don't think any of the players expected much of the new boy. We accepted that he would play an emergency role at fullback. If he kicked a few goals, that would be a bonus. In the event Jarrett's debut was sensational. He scored 19 points, equalling Jack Bancroft's fifty-seven-year-old record for Wales, and in the process he became the first Welsh fullback since Vivian Jenkins to score a try.

We knew that England, on that fine spring day in Cardiff, with a hard-baked ground, would pepper Jarrett with high kicks. With his complete lack of positional experience he seemed an obvious weakness in our defence. A seasoned campaigner would have enjoyed the challenge; but in the Welsh camp we were aware that if the slightest lack of confidence was revealed, then our task would be that much more difficult.

In one sense I was happy to see Keith selected. This was only my second match for Wales and my first at the Arms Park. My excitement and euphoria had hardly abated, and although the pressure was still present, it had slightly eased since Jarrett now received most of the media attention. It must have been a positively frightening experience for him, straight out of school, playing at the Arms Park and in an unaccustomed position.

It was, of course, important that he should feel comfortable as soon as possible and that he should get an early chance to show his kicking ability. I was only just getting over my own introduction to the heady atmosphere of playing at Cardiff – it was all so quick and frantic, desperate sometimes: those youthful dreams and imaginary schoolboy matches against England had suddenly become reality. If I felt on a razor's edge, I can't imagine what Keith endured, particularly in the opening minutes when the sound, the atmosphere of the Arms Park engulfs you and seems to swallow you up.

Still, we had hopes of a reasonable performance because, against all predictions, we had given a good account of ourselves in Paris against France in our previous match. Caution tempered our optimism though, for as the pessimists rightly pointed out we also faced a fifth successive defeat. Then there was the added pressure that England were bidding for the Triple Crown, which meant that they had a pretty good team.

In a sense, all the doubts, the questions and the answers seemed to hinge on Jarrett's first kick at goal. If he missed, it would not only be a big personal setback, but the rest of us would dip our heads and the struggle would become psychological rather than physical. In the event, Jarrett's first kick was an epic. It did not matter that it flicked over from a post; the fact that it went over sent a surge of adrenalin through the whole side. It gave us the positive attitude we were looking for.

Almost at once we started winning quality possession and England were under the cosh, having to cope with the pressure. Keith, suffice to say, was having a stormer of a match. Although his positional play gave some of us a few moments of anxiety, he seemed to lead a charmed life. It was as if he could do no wrong.

Even so, England were only 4 points adrift into the second half, when Colin McFadyean kicked to the open side under the north stand. Jarrett raced up and fielded comfortably. There were immediately many options open to him. He decided, incredibly, to run and, with gasps of astonishment all round, he raced around the fringe of the English defence, sprinting home for a marvellous 50-metre try. The Arms Park erupted. The applause was no less resounding when moments later he converted the try with a magnificent kick from the touchline. Another four conversions and a penalty and he had written himself into history. And to think we were worried about his confidence!

It amounted, of course, to the most remarkable debut in the history of the championship. Phil Judd, England's captain, summed up the visitors' anguish. 'I never thought I'd see the day when England would score 21 points at Cardiff and still end up on the losing side.' It is another measure of Jarrett's contribution that England's 21 points were their biggest haul in forty-four championship matches in Wales.

Delighted as we all were with Keith's success in that match, it was also poignantly the last championship match for two of Wales's outstanding players, Dai Watkins and Dewi Bebb, one of my schoolboy heroes. On my very first visit to the Arms Park, on 17 January 1959, I had watched Dewi score the winning try against England. In many ways Dewi's debut was similar to Jarrett's. A virtually unknown North Walian with only a handful of matches to his credit, the responsibility on his shoulders must have been similar to that borne by Keith. Dewi coped all right, back in 1959, and on thirty-three further appearances for Wales.

I had watched Bebb score his first try for Wales, and here, on this his final appearance, I was a little nearer to applaud his eleventh and last one. I made sure that I snatched up the match ball to give it to Dewi, which was as much a sentimental gesture as anything for it had been Dewi who had presented me with the match ball after my debut against France. When he did so, he knew all about the pressures and subsequent precious memories of one's first appearance. The ball ensured I would never forget it. The habit of collecting match balls, by the way, has stuck. It has now become an Edwards trademark.

After all that Jarrett achieved, the remainder of the match seems of little significance. I was happy enough that things had gone well personally – I had concentrated successfully on keeping my passes short and accurate for Dai Watkins – and the forwards had had a fine match. My pal Gerald Davies had helped himself to two tries and Billy Raybould dropped a goal.

But what did all that matter? This was, in every sense, Keith Jarrett's match.

Wales: K. S. Jarrett; S. J. Watkins, W. H. Raybould, T. G. R. Davies, D. I. E. Bebb; D. Watkins (captain), G. O. Edwards; D. Williams, N. R. Gale, D. J. Lloyd, B. Price, W. T. Mainwaring, R. E. Jones, J. Taylor, W. D. Morris

England: R. W. Hosen; K. F. Savage, R. D. Hearn, C. W. McFadyean, R. E. Webb; J. F. Finlan, R. D. A. Pickering; P. E. Judd (captain), S. B. Richards, M. J. Coulman, J.

Barton, D. E. J. Watt, D. P. Rogers, R. B. Taylor, D. M. Rollitt

Referee: D. C. J. McMahon (Scotland)

## Wales 30 England 9, Cardiff Arms Park, 12 April 1969

England arrived at Cardiff understandably buoyant if not confident after two good victories over France and Scotland, but having been beaten by Ireland. Wales, in contrast, had their sights on the championship and the Triple Crown for, although having been held 8–8 by France in Paris, Scotland and Ireland had been accounted for. A glittering prize beckoned.

England had made one change from the side which had defeated Scotland 8–3 at Twickenham, Ken Plummer coming in for Keith Fielding. It was Ken's first cap – and he'll remember it all his life for, on this day of history-making, fate appointed him to play opposite Maurice Richards. Maurice turned in one of the most devastating scoring performances of all time by running in four tries. Previously only the immortal Willie Llewellyn in 1899 and Reggie Gibbs in 1908 had scored four tries for Wales. In my view Maurice should have been a regular in the Welsh side much longer than he was. In fact, he played only a paltry six championship matches – and this one was his last, for he succumbed to the lure of playing for cash, along with Keith Jarrett, our 19-point hero against England in 1967. What a great loss to Welsh rugby was that dual defection. Jarrett won ten caps and I believe was a vastly underrated player, accomplished as he was in both defence and attack. And, of course, he could kick as well!

I knew Maurice very well, for he was my team-mate at

Cardiff. One hesitates to describe a fellow-player as brilliant, but that's what Maurice was. Off the field, Maurice was a gentle, introspective person, but on the paddock he was completely different, hunting with all the dedication and ruthlessness of a forest animal. He was both an elusive and a powerful, aggressive runner, and what marked him as a player apart was his innate ability to beat an opponent in a variety of ways – side-step, swerve or sheer speed. I have come up against many fine wings. Maurice Richards was one of the greatest.

No one in that Welsh side was surprised when Maurice scored four tries against England. He was capable of that in any match, which was another measure of his ability. But what must be remembered is that Maurice's bonanza was only part of the story. The creativity, the setting-up of his tries, came from others in this well-balanced Welsh side, who made optimum use of the possession they gained. Two important cogs in the machine were as yet in the novice class, in an international sense – J. P. R. Williams and Mervyn Davies. This was their first season for Wales, but even in those early days they displayed the composure and assurance of seasoned internationals.

Added to this, Barry John and I had, as they say, begun to settle down as a partnership. Our play began to assume an authority based on an intuitive understanding. At least, Barry acquainted me with what type of service he wanted and when!

Much has been made of the tendency at the time of the Welsh selectors to play a sort of Russian roulette with the captaincy, with John Dawes, Brian Price and me. Brian had been given the job that season and I was a sort of unofficial vice-captain. As scrum half, it was reckoned that I was in the best position to be in charge of the backs and could control tactics behind the scrum. This plan would have been adopted but for the fact that Brian had to drop out because of injury. His match against France a month earlier was to be his last for Wales. I remember the disappointment I felt at the time that Brian had pulled out. He was playing as well as he had ever done. Naturally, I was extremely pleased to take over as captain – particularly against England – and there was ample compensation in that Brian's line-out duties were allocated to a sinewy stripling from Llanelli, Delme Thomas. In the second row with Delme was the big feller, Brian Thomas, and between them they had the task of containing the highly regarded English pair, Nigel Horton and Peter Larter. Suffice to say, 'Twmws' finished his Wales career in style and made many worthy contributions to our success.

My chief concern on the day was not to become over-involved in the play and to concentrate on getting our backs away. We had so much good possession – especially from the Thomas boys in the middle and Mervyn Davies at the tail of the line-outs – that in the end the match had become the most satisfying that I'd ever had with Barry. I truly enjoyed every moment of it.

Since returning from the Lions tour of South Africa in 1968, my passing had improved markedly, largely because I was more confident. I modelled myself on Chris Laidlaw and Ken Catchpole by adopting the spin pass and manipulating it to suit my own requirements. A lot of misinformed comments were made about this improvement in my pass; even former players said that my passing was so long that the wings were running into touch on the other side of the field! It's true that in South Africa Barry and I had practised a lot, but there was never a conscious effort to improve my pass as such. People had the wrong idea about that pass. What they didn't realize was that the long pass was employed as a tactical weapon. Not every pass had great length. Much depended on Barry. If a flanker was bearing directly down on him, I would give him the longer pass so that he could run alongside it and then use the ball to skim outside the flanker. Eventually we developed what could be described as a telepathic understanding. I didn't have to look where Barry was – I knew exactly where he'd be. That's really what determined the length of the pass.

As I have suggested, the wealth of line-out ball we received in the match provided the platform for the victory. It wasn't just a question of the jumping: Jeff Young's throwing-in was not fully appreciated by most observers at the time; and it was not long, either, before Delme proved himself one of the finest line-out exponents I have ever played with. Nowadays they call them tap-backs; in my day they were deflections, and Delme's were so accurate that invariably I was into my pass very quickly. Little time was lost and I had yards in which to move. In the largeness of a match, these are small ingredients. But they are very important in establishing which side has the edge, and are often overlooked by the critics.

At the time I was not exactly seeing eye to eye with the critics. I had been accused of being too individual and of wasting a lot of ball. As everything was going so well, there was a temptation for me to justify some of that criticism! But the match was much more important than that. It was crucial in my development as a player because I consciously disciplined my play as never before. My normal brash, impetuous self was put under wraps; I only took on the opposition to set up colleagues. The approach seemed to rub off on the rest of the team and, in every sense, we produced a real team performance in which every player worked for everyone else. As the match unfolded, so our confidence built, and I think every Welsh player realized that, given the opportunities, we could produce an outstanding performance. We certainly had the players to seize any advantage.

Although the half-time score was 3–3, it flattered England and disguised our superiority up front. Two penalties by Jarrett gave us the required leverage, and once we had our noses in front we worked for one more score which we were confident would open up the floodgates. It came from Barry John, a crushing blow for England as he weaved through their defence with all his imperious skill.

A few seasons previously, that would have been the signal for every one to try to get in on the act, to the detriment of the team effort. But this 1969 side was different. It possessed a tremendous attitude and worked in unison to score four more beautifully conceived and executed tries. It didn't matter that Maurice Richards scored the lot and justifiably dominated the headlines. The credit belonged to each and every one of us; there was a corporate glow of satisfaction that moves we had practised and thought about in training had come off in such spectacular fashion. It might be going a little far to suggest we felt sorry for the principal victim of Maurice's plunder – let's say we had some sympathy for Ken Plummer.

Naturally I was proud to have captained a Wales side which won the Triple Crown. But the most satisfying aspect of it, really, was that we had done it in style. That, coupled with what seemed at the time to be my answer to the critics, made the match one of the most memorable of my career.

Wales: J. P. R. Williams; S. J. Watkins, K. S. Jarrett, S. J. Dawes, M. C. R. Richards; B. John, G. O. Edwards (captain); D. Williams, J. Young, D. J. Lloyd, W. D. Thomas, B. E. Thomas, W. D. Morris, J. Taylor, T. M. Davies

England: R. Hiller; K. C. Plummer, J. S. Spencer, D. J. Duckham, R. E. Webb; J. F. Finlan, T. C. Wintle; D. L.

Powell, J. V. Pullin, K. E. Fairbrother, N. E. Horton, P. J. Larter, R. B. Taylor, D. P. Rogers (captain), D. M. Rollitt

Referee: D. P. d'Arcy (Ireland)

## England 6 Wales 9, Twickenham, 4 February 1978

This was a match I shall remember for ever – or, to be more precise, it was the occasion rather than the dogged eighty minutes of a championship match. Its specialness for me was that I was making my fiftieth appearance for Wales, and while other memories flood and recede, this will always have pride of place. It was, simply, a lovely, emotional day, obviously not only for me but for countless others who signified their wish to be associated with a landmark in Welsh rugby history with a stream of good wishes and telegrams. I was totally overwhelmed. My colleagues in the Welsh team were marvellous too: they acknowledged that I was unwittingly the centre of attention, but even so, each in his own way wanted to make the day memorable for me. A straightforward handshake, a 'Well done' or 'Congratulations, Gareth' meant a great deal, although not as much as the good wishes which, because of the curious self-conscious nature of rugby players, largely went unspoken. There are some things you do not need to say, but you appreciate them because you know instinctively that they are being thought.

It was a nice touch too when the boys hung back as we ran out onto the pitch, leaving me in the forefront as I led out the team on my last appearance at Twickenham. The England players too were not slow to offer their congratulations on the landmark.

Having often been a critic of the governors of the game, I

might say I felt a little humble, if not suitably chastised, when at the after-match banquet the Rugby Football Union presented me with a beautiful Spode bowl. It was the fiftieth and therefore the last of the fifty commissioned for the RFU Centenary in 1971, and as such will remain one of the most treasured of my possessions.

What the RFU can do, of course, the WRU will try to improve upon. They marked the occasion later in the year by presenting me with a second cap, an honour bestowed on no other Welsh player. The cap was embroidered with all the matches in which I played, the number 50 emblazoned on the front. That, of course, remains a very special possession too.

It is a pity that the match itself did little to warm spectators on a cold, wet February afternoon. The best that can be said of the Welsh performance was that it was hard and workmanlike. A good England pack defeated and frustrated most of our best intentions, and we had to rely upon Phil Bennett's place kicking to gain the first notch in what was to be a Triple Crown and Grand Slam season.

Phil remembers the occasion very well, although for different reasons from mine. He told me years later that when Wales were awarded a penalty kick, after Alistair Hignell had kicked two to put England in front, he was overwhelmed by offers from Stevie Fenwick, Allan Martin and others to take it. 'I'll have a go,' he was told. The ball was heavy and wet, but Phil declined, as he did later in the match when he was presented with another opportunity, the kick this time enabling Wales to draw level. Then, towards the end, when Wales were awarded yet another kick, this time a comparatively easy one from 25 metres, and much more crucial for it meant winning or losing the match, none of the would-be kickers were to be seen. 'I looked around,' said Phil, 'and there was not one of the b—s about. They'd all retired to the halfway line. They all wanted to be heroes, but not when it really mattered.' It is now history that Phil took the kick and it flew home, leaving Wales the victors.

One of those three penalties was conceded because of offside by Bob Mordell, the Rosslyn Park flanker who was making his debut for England, along with Paul Dodge, John Horton and my Cardiff club-mate, Barry Nelmes. Poor Mordell never played for England again.

Another for whom this was a last championship match was the referee, Norman Sanson, although he officiated at two other England matches, both against New Zealand, before he quit, disillusioned with the international scene. Sanson's departure was, in my view, a serious loss to the game, for along with Ireland's Paddy d'Arcy, he was definitely one of the best international referees.

A lot of referees perform on the international field out of a sense of duty, it seems to me, rather than for any real regard for what is required. Some stick too rigidly to the letter of the law; and many of them have been responsible for alienation, if not total resentment, among the players. Sanson was certainly not one of these. Not only did he understand the game well, but what endeared him to the players was his clarity in decision-making, his consistency and his fairness. People have assumed that because he had a reputation for strictness and was unhesitating in sending off players for foul play, the players did not like him. That was not true. He was widely respected.

How different indeed from some referees. After a Lions match, one South African referee answered our criticism with, 'I've got to live here' – the response of several other overseas referees who have shown bias against visiting sides.

I got to know Sanson extremely well during Wales's tour of Japan in 1973 when he accompanied the party as a 'neutral' referee. As part of the tour, as it were, it would have been understandable had he leaned in favour of Wales when he refereed. But he did not, not once, and his honesty and open-handedness were appreciated by every one of us.

England: A. J. Hignell; P. J. Squires, B. J. Corless, P. W. Dodge, M. A. C. Slemen; J. P. Horton, M. Young; B. G. Nelmes, P. J. Wheeler, M. A. Burton, W. B. Beaumont (captain), N. E. Horton, R. J. Mordell, M. Rafter, J. P. Scott

Wales: J. P. R. Williams; T. G. R. Davies, R. W. R. Gravell, S. P. Fenwick, J. J. Williams; P. Bennett (captain), G. O. Edwards; G. Price, R. W. Windsor, A. G. Faulkner, A. J. Martin, G. A. D. Wheel, J. Squire, T. J. Cobner, D. L. Quinnell

Referee: N. R. Sanson (Scotland)

# 2 Wales *versus* Scotland

As international venues, Cardiff and Edinburgh have one special thing in common. On match day, the entire centre of each city seems to succumb to the all-embracing euphoria of the occasion. The colour, the noise and the expectation flow along Cardiff's main thoroughfares – Westgate Street, St Mary Street and Queen Street – and in Edinburgh, it is Princes Street, Rose Street and the road leading out of the centre to Murrayfield which somehow become, for the day, a great rugby eisteddfodic festival.

I know of Welsh rugby fans who have never been to Twickenham, Lansdowne Road or Parc des Princes, but religiously scrimp and save 50p pieces so that they can embark upon one of rugby's great journeys – the Murrayfield Pilgrimage. There is no obvious answer as to why the Murrayfield match is held in such high esteem by the Welsh, or why they throng the Scottish capital in their thousands every two years. What is certain is that the Scottish welcome and generosity play an important part in making it unarguably the favourite outing for the Welsh rugby supporter. No sooner has one trip finished than the ritualistic planning for the next is undertaken. Some go time after time to the same place, the same hotel, the same guest house. Others believe that variety is the spice of life and sample Scottish hospitality from the Borders to the Highlands before descending upon Edinburgh on match day. When they get there, they find the advance parties already milling through the avenues and streets, some of whom have been 'getting the flavour' of this beautiful city for up to five days. Then finally come the late arrivals, willing victims of the 'Suicide Special', the overloaded train which leaves Wales on Friday and travels through the night and spills everyone out next morning, haggard and bleary-eyed. Heroes to a man! There are others too who set out with honest intention and get no farther than the Welsh–English border where acceptable compensation is gained in the television room of a sympathetic hostelry.

In 1975 the invasion peaked when an estimated 35,000 drove, flew and hitch-hiked to swell the Murrayfield attendance to a world record 104,000. Ground-control regulations will never allow such a massive crowd again – but that will not prevent the two-year exodus. They'd have to close down Murrayfield to stop the Welsh rugby man travelling up to Scotland.

On the morning of the Scotland–Wales match in Edinburgh, it is always reassuring as a player to open your bedroom window at the Welsh team headquarters, the North British Hotel, and behold the magnificent sight of the red and white throng noisily streaming this way and that outside the hotel. For them, it seems a homage, this attendance at the Welsh team hotel. When I first went to Scotland I used to join the crowd, mixing and chatting and joking, hoping that the atmosphere, the good-luck wishes and that indomitable Welsh humour would help get the ticker going. But in reality it was torture. The well-meaning Welsh fan would back-slap you to death, given the chance. Still, the sight of them from the hotel will always generate that feeling of being part of something special, time-honoured and traditional.

The drive in the team coach to Murrayfield, too, is unvarying in its stimulation and excitement. Gerald Davies and I used to sit next to each other and soak up the *hwyl* as we sped by the hundreds sitting at the roadside, munching their pies and sandwiches, and drinking their beer from cans. 'Got any spare tickets, boys?' some would shout. No joke, really. A lot of them were ticketless. They had come on the pilgrimage, but there were not many miracles performed on the road to the Murrayfield shrine.

When we alighted at the ground, there were others waiting, eyes whisky-glazed, standing to attention or proffering advice and good wishes for our battle ahead. 'Give 'em hell, boys.' 'Now don't let us down, lads.' 'I've got a week's wages riding on this one, Gar.' 'Buy you a brewery tonight, boys, if you win.' As the years roll by, much in rugby changes. But not those fans or their comments. I suppose by the end I had become accustomed to it. It did not stop me turning to Gerald and saying, 'Can't let them down, can we, Ger?'

Promising not to let them down is one thing; achieving it, particularly at Murrayfield, is another. The Scots, in their own backyard, are whipping boys for no one. They have always been redoubtable opposition, battling to the last minute to hold on to their gains, or trying to snatch the victory from their visitors. I played five times at Murrayfield and was on the winning side three times. Every match was tense and tenaciously fought. Thank goodness we had rather the better of it when we played them at Cardiff.

## Wales 5 Scotland 0, Cardiff Arms Park, 3 February 1968

I was a 'veteran' of four internationals when appointed captain of Wales for this match. I was told that I was to be the successor to Norman Gale by Tony Lewis, a friend and former England cricket captain, at a dinner in Cardiff. I was initially incredulous, and it took a few swift bevvies before the news sank in. The doubts, the apprehension started immediately. Not even Bill Samuel, who guided my rugby career from start to finish, could alleviate my anxiety when he told me, 'You were destined for it.'

The captaincy, although an honour, was fraught with problems of self-analysis, but my biggest sense of unease, at twenty years and seven months old, was in facing up to some of the older warriors in the Welsh side. To some extent the selectors made that particular confrontation less daunting by announcing six changes from the side which had drawn 11–11 at Twickenham the previous month. Some experienced campaigners had been axed, and although we were not given any hint as to their intentions, the selectors had plumped for a comparatively young side to take on the Scots.

Certainly, I had no qualms about leading the threequarters, since Barry, Keri Jones and Gerald were all club-mates, good friends and counsellors. Still, I felt at the time that there were some strange selections in this Welsh team, but what concerned me most was that in order to become a successful captain there was only one matter of importance – gaining victory. History books devote little space to losers. Wales had already been soundly beaten by New Zealand the previous November, and that defeat inevitably had thrown team planning and preparation into some confusion. A number of the 'survivors' were comparatively green as international players, lacking the composure which accompanies experience and which breeds confidence. But I was fortunate to have had some measure of success as a captain of the East Wales side which played the All Blacks, which was, I suppose, a factor in my nomination as skipper of Wales. By the time the team had been shuffled from the All Black defeat to facing up to Scotland, I was one of the more seasoned members.

One of my biggest worries was my pre-match team talk

although, as all international captains quickly realize, there is no better motivator in the dressing room than the jersey hanging on the wall. It is its own inducement. Our jerseys, though, weren't hanging there waiting for us. They were handed out individually by Gerry Lewis, the team physiotherapist, with a knowing smile and a 'good luck' wish. I got into the habit of kissing my jersey every time it was handed to me. My team talk on this occasion I find hard to recall, although I do remember one of the touch judges being fairly impressed.

Wales badly needed a victory to restore confidence after the draw with England and the All Black defeat. Fortunately, tradition was on our side: Scotland found winning in Wales very difficult. They had beaten us at home only three times since 1929 and only once in the previous eleven visits.

The match, as it turned out, was an undistinguished one, but a Welsh victory for all that. Keri Jones scored a try early in the first half, finishing off a move which some observers criticized as containing a forward pass. Keith Jarrett, who had helped create the try, converted it, and that was the only score of the whole eighty minutes. But a win is a win for a' that, and as far as I was concerned the only thing that mattered was that we had a victory under our belts.

The most contentious issue turned out to be whether the captaincy had affected my game. The arguments raged then – and still do! A small publishing industry was established in Wales devoted to whether I was influenced by having the captaincy thrust upon me. The argument misses the basic point. When I was first appointed captain, Wales were in the throes of transition. The players barely knew each other and coaching was only just becoming acceptable. Eleven changes in three matches did not materially affect my position as captain. I felt I did the job to the best of my ability, and I can state unequivocally that the captaincy did not affect the way in which I played or my attitude to the job of scrum half. If anything did affect my game in those early days, it was a mixture of youth and anxiety, not the captaincy.

Wales: D. Rees; S. J. Watkins, K. S. Jarrett, T. G. R. Davies, W. K. Jones; B. John, G. O. Edwards (captain); D. J. Lloyd, J. Young, J. P. O'Shea, M. Wiltshire, W. D. Thomas, W. D. Morris, A. J. Gray, R. E. Jones

Scotland: S. Wilson; A. J. W. Hinshelwood, J. W. C. Turner, J. N. M. Frame, G. J. Keith; D. H. Chisholm, A. J. Hastie; A. B. Carmichael, F. A. L. Laidlaw, D. M. D. Rollo, P. K. Stagg, G. W. E. Mitchell, J. P. Fisher (captain), T. G. Elliot, A. H. W. Boyle

Referee: G. C. Lamb (England)

## Scotland 18 Wales 19, Murrayfield, 6 February 1971

The all-conquering Welsh team of the early seventies had taken about three years to create and mature, rising phoenix-fashion from the ashes of the disastrous tour of New Zealand in 1969, which undoubtedly hastened the arrival of a new school of thinking in Welsh rugby. It must also be reiterated that the cornerstone of what amounted to the Welsh revival came in the shape of the vision and composure of John Dawes, the London Welsh captain of that time. The impassioned flair of Clive Rowlands appealing to our Nonconformist consciences had been replaced by an outward calm, although other important factors were that Barry and I had played together for a long international period; that J.P.R. had added a new dimension to attacking fullback play; and that our forwards, full of confidence, were a match for any opposition.

We were now equipped to deal with most situations. In 1971 Wales had one of the best teams it has been my privilege to watch, since that is what I did at times. There were so many admirable qualities in that side. And never was their character, their ability and confidence put to a greater test than against Scotland at Murrayfield in February 1971.

We had arrived in Scotland on a high after hammering England 22–6 at the Arms Park. Scotland had kept the side which somewhat unluckily had lost 8–13 to France at Stade Colombes. The pundits, however, did not rate the Scots. Very few newspapers forecast any sort of chance for them, which no doubt added to their motivation. They were raring to go as soon as they emerged from the tunnel. In contrast Wales possessed a quiet confidence. As history shows, it turned out to be the match of a lifetime.

Peter Brown, Scotland's captain, was one of the most annoying international goal kickers I ever came across. No doubt this annoyance was accentuated by his high success rate, but everything he did when it came to place kicking looked awkward, even ugly. Peter would turn his back to the ball, turn again and thump away, unfussed and with no sense, or so it seemed, of direction or distance. Invariably kicks which looked certain to snap the corner flags crept over the bar, and the fact that he got away with it so outrageously, so often, irritated me. In the match he rekindled Scotland's hopes with four penalty goals, all of them converted with remarkable economy. They remain the greatest number of penalties by Scotland in any match against Wales.

Although Wales led 8–6 at half time, the Scots clawed their way back and, as they did, each score generated a fresh supply of enthusiasm. I was nevertheless convinced when I scored a try which gave us a 5-point lead, that another 3 points, no matter how achieved, would bury the Scots, dirks, claymores and all. The redoubtable Sandy Carmichael dismissed such premature confidence when he hurled himself from a line-out and crashed over for a try. Peter Brown missed the conversion but added to our frustration by coming back to land a penalty to restore Scotland's lead.

It was the best possible test of the resilience of this Welsh side. It is not with hindsight that I remained convinced that we were still going to win. We had a side of many gifted players who had built up an understanding. The greatest asset, however, was composure. Barry John glided through for one of his special tries and the Welsh 'army' on the Murrayfield slopes rejoiced yet again. Did that finish Scotland? No sooner had we nosed ahead than Scotland tore back at us. Peter Brown, yet again, kicked a penalty and Chris Rea scored a try to give them a 18–14 lead with the match in its dying moments.

It was incredible that defeat was ominously so near. We had played well, had done more than enough to survive and salvage a result. Against this the Scots were magnificent. They refused to accept any idea that they would lose and produced a display which defied all predictions. In the second half they were much more highly motivated than Wales and kept posing questions which we failed to answer.

As we resignedly retired behind the goal line for Peter's conversion, everybody wanted to know how much time was left. I suspect there was in the Welsh team at that moment some sense of outrage, even anger, that we found ourselves down and almost out.

'How long is there to go, Syd?' someone asked John Dawes.

'Plenty of time,' replied Dawes. 'There's got to be six or seven minutes left.'

If John had not said that, for all its obvious exaggeration, there is a possibility that we might have panicked. As it was, there wasn't one of us who did not know that there were at most a couple of minutes left on Mike Titcomb's watch. What Dawes had calculated, of course, was that there was still time to pull off a great rescue act and to set light to the touchpaper. What happened in those dying seconds of the match has been acclaimed as among the greatest moments in Welsh rugby history. Fascinatingly, even the Scots had a sense of foreboding. Frank Laidlaw, their hooker, said to me after the match, 'Do you know, Gareth, even when Chris Rea scored his try and Peter kicked the penalty, and we had a 4-point lead . . . I still felt we were going to lose.'

Curiously, I shared Frank's view, because even with time running out I still had confidence in this Welsh side, although I admit that confidence was a little frayed as the seconds ticked away. We needed one big effort and everyone, to a man, lifted himself for just one more assault to try to snatch the match back. Down we went to the Scots' 25-metre line, with them to throw in. There might have been a little desperation, even panic, in their ranks because unaccountably they got into an awful mix-up over their line-out signal. Gordon Brown, his brother Peter and scrum half Paterson were at the heart of the tangle. Whatever the call was and wherever the ball was supposed to have gone, it went to Delme Thomas at the front of the line and he palmed it down beautifully to me. It was a bonus with a capital B. We moved the ball quickly along the line – no tricks, no dummies or intricate ploys – to Gerald for him to move into overdrive and cross at the corner . . . 17–18! The conversion would win us the match.

It might seem ungenerous in retrospect, but I have to say that at the time I didn't have much confidence in the choice of kicker for this crucial conversion. When Barry or Phil Bennett were with you in the side, picking a place kicker was never a problem. In 1971, however, Barry was not crowned 'King' because of his awesome accuracy with the boot, and

Phil's time was yet to come. J.P.R. and I fancied ourselves as modern-day Don Clarkes, but our talent was ignored as John Dawes threw the ball instead to his London Welsh clubmate, John Taylor. 'Bas' Taylor was a natural left-footer and something of a Cool Hand Luke character.

Back on the halfway line, we were anything but cool as Taylor went towards his mark. We were all on edge. Delme Thomas was in a frenzy.

'*Gar, allai byth a edrych.*' ('Gar, I can't watch.')

'*Meddylia bo ni wed dod yr holl ffordd lan fan hyn, sgori tair gwaith, a colli.*' ('Just think of it, all this way, score three tries and lose.')

'*Gar, allai byth a edrych.*' ('Gar, I can't watch.')

'*Ol reit, edrycha i te.*' ('OK, I'll watch for both of us then.')

The kick seemed a long, long way out. But John, unflustered and seemingly not in the slightest concerned, took only the minimum time to prepare his tee and position the ball.

'*Mae hi'n mynd, mae hi yn ddigon uchel . . . mae hi'n troi mewn. DEL! Myn uffarn I, mae e wedi cichio hi!*' ('Basil Brush' John Taylor had done the job.)

Murrayfield erupted. John's kick went over and Wales had won. The most incredible ending to any match. But, wait, there was still time. In fact, more time than any of us realized and the match was still alive, with all the possibilities yet again of Scotland coming back at us. It was nerve-wracking.

We decided we simply had to stay in Scotland's half. I even attempted a dropped goal during those frenzied last moments. At last, after what seemed an eternity, Mike Titcomb blew for no-side.

'Never in doubt,' some wag suggested as we trooped off wearily.

Someone who wouldn't have appreciated the joke was the Welsh coach, Clive Rowlands. Clive couldn't bear to watch as Bas ran up to take his kick.

Clive didn't mind when we unceremoniously threw him fully clothed into the team bath. It might seem a funny way of congratulating someone . . . but Clive deserved much of the credit for our victory.

He had ranted and raved about our Welsh 'tickers', reminding all of us of our responsibility, how important it was to every living Welshman, of what it meant to our fathers, mothers, uncles, aunts, brothers, sisters, ministers and teachers. No one was left out when Clive Rowlands gave his pre-match pep talk. 'They talk about the Murrayfield bogey,' he had shouted at us. 'What *bloody* bogey? They've only beaten us once up here in twelve years! Bogey? It's their bogey, not ours!' As he emerged dripping from the bath, laughing like a Cheshire Cat, we all thought about what he had said. He went round us all, thanking each of us for our efforts. There were tears in his eyes. Who said rugby was only a game?

On reflection, it was curious that we had made such heavy weather of that victory at Murrayfield, particularly since our team contained so much varied talent. It was a team which effectively picked itself: J.P.R. at fullback was bravery personified; John Bevan was so powerful and thrustful on the wing that I was relieved he was a Cardiff and Wales club-mate; Ian Hall and John Dawes (and later Roy Bergiers and Arthur Lewis) were all high-quality footballers who could time a pass and draw a man, which made life so much more attractive for our wings. And, of course, one of our wings was the best there was, someone who could create so much out of so little, and who scored such tries as to have us all standing applauding as he whipped over the line. Gerald Davies was the supreme footballer. He'd have scored a lot more tries had we given him more of the ball, that's for sure. Then there was Barry John – 'You throw it and I'll catch it.' What can I say or add that others have not already waxed long and lyrically. Perhaps only he possessed that unique ability to make time stand still, or to spread a second into an eternity so that he gave himself time and space when all around him was frantic and furious.

I don't think the back-row talents of Mervyn Davies, John Taylor and Dai Morris were ever fully appreciated in Wales, certainly not while they were playing as a unit. Taylor was criticized for being too short, Mervyn had to work hard in order to become accepted, and there were those who thought Dai lacked finesse. To my mind, they ranked among the best. I have only seen one better back row, that of Greyling, Ellis and Bedford, of South Africa. Mervyn, Dai and John complemented each other in every sense. Dai was a gift of a forward for a scrum half – 'Shadow', as he was called, would have done the FBI proud. His uncanny ability to be in the right place, taking the ball on and sustaining a movement, invariably meant that Wales were going forward into the breakdown. Added to that were the ball-winning and destructive qualities of Mervyn, who never gave less than total commitment in a Welsh jersey. John provided the quickness and finesse – and did a lot of Barry's tackling!

Scotland: I. S. G. Smith; W. C. C. Steele, J. N. M. Frame, C. W. W. Rea, A. G. Biggar; J. W. C. Turner, D. S. Paterson; I. McLauchlan, F. A. L. Laidlaw, A. B. Carmichael, A. F. McHarg, G. L. Brown, N. A. MacEwan, R. J. Arneil, P. C. Brown (captain)

Wales: J. P. R. Williams; T. G. R. Davies, S. J. Dawes (captain), I. Hall, J. C. Bevan; B. John, G. O. Edwards; D. B. Llewelyn, J. Young, D. Williams, W. D. Thomas, M. G. Roberts, W. D. Morris, J. Taylor, T. M. Davies

Referee: M. H. Titcomb (England)

## Wales 35 Scotland 12, Cardiff Arms Park, 5 February 1972

Bill Samuel, my old gym teacher, was a man of many talents, crystal-ball gazing among them. 'You haven't scored from the halfway line, yet, Gareth,' he said, as if that was a novel idea. What it was, of course, was another challenge, artfully put to me so that, if the opportunity ever arose, I would be awake to it. At the time it was suggested, I didn't give it much thought or serious consideration. But events proved that that man Samuel not only knew a thing about the game, but was even skilled in prediction.

Wales had got off to a good start in the 1972 championship by beating England 12–3 at Twickenham. The Scots were our next opponents, at the Arms Park, and they showed little respect for tradition with a first-half display of verve and drive which earned them a half-time lead of 12–10. It was customary for Wales to get off to a slow start. It was almost as if we wanted to witness what the opposition had to offer, before lifting our own game accordingly. Despite their brisk start, the Scots had missed a few opportunities, their movements faltering at a crucial stage when we were literally on the run.

It was against this backcloth that Bill Samuel's 'prediction' came true. The score probably turned the game decisively. We were deep inside our own half and won some untidy possession at a line-out. Mervyn Davies did the housework and popped the ball up to me from the tail of the line-out as I approached him in full stride. Had I been static I would probably have looked around for Barry, but I was committed to my run on the short side – and, what is more, I could see an opening. Off I went confidently for I had spotted that Roger Arneil, Scotland's flanker, had moved just a fraction too wide to have any chance of picking me off. By this time

I had travelled, say, 10 metres, par for the course, and I started to look around for 'Shadow' Morris. He was nowhere to be seen. It was a strange feeling, to say the least, to be out running in the open without the omnipresent Morris ready to take my pass, tuck it under his arm and charge onwards. Where on earth are you, Dai, I asked myself. Instantly I realized that I was really on my own and that my break had caught everyone off guard, including my team-mates. I have since watched the move on television and realized just how astonished the crowd were, because, of course, they had a better view of things than me! It was a tremendous sensation suddenly to feel free and full of running – though I admit to a couple of backward glances in the first 30–40 metres. No one, however, had come remotely near me, though I fully expected that at any moment a defender would bolt in from an unsighted angle and bundle me into touch. I consoled myself that if that happened at least it had been a good run and had taken Wales out of a potentially vulnerable position. The crowd would have acknowledged that, if not the press boys!

The first defender I actually saw was Arthur Brown, the Gala fullback. Arthur hovered near the 25-metre line, but he seemed to be stationary and standing too deep to present a problem, as I was now really motoring. When at last Arthur decided to move in on me, I waited until the last possible moment before kicking over his head. My training as a high hurdler now served me well for I didn't even have to break stride to chase on past Arthur and after the ball. The fact that I had managed to maintain speed proved crucial because by now the Scottish defence had been remarshalled and coverers were homing in on me from behind. It was now that Lady Luck favoured me. As the ball bounced, it curved towards me. All this was happening at breakneck speed and it called for a snap decision – should I try to pick the ball up or flip it to one of my supporting Welsh players. There is an argument that everything you do on the rugby field is instinctive, impulsive; but at international level the prevailing instinct is not to make a mistake. At this level, often it is not what you do, but what you don't do that counts. In the event, I knew that given a little luck and recalling my soccer skills I could probably tap the ball with my boot and steer it over the goal line. By this time my run had swallowed 70 metres of the pitch and I could hear the roars of the crowd with every stride. The ball raced ahead of me, over the try line and threatened to run on, disastrously over the dead-ball line. For a split second I panicked. If the ball went dead, the whole effort of the run would have been wasted, remembered momentarily by those who watched it, but soon forgotten. I prayed that the ball would slow or just stop and sit up, but it began to veer towards touch-in-goal. Panic again, as Lewis Dick, haring in from the other side of the field, was now challenging for the fateful race to be first to the ball. I knew that Lewis, who had come on as a replacement for the injured Alistair Biggar, was faster, but if determination was going to count, he would have to come second this time. Often I've seen wings go for the line but lack the killer instinct at the vital moment. It is always better to go for the line with a dive. That way your body acts as a shield and there is very little a tackler can do to stop the score.

Well, all this was happening at such a pace that it didn't take me long to decide what had to be done. As the ball skimmed across the try line it was a question of now or never. I dived in after it, grounded it and then everything went red.

Gerald was first there to pick me up.

'*Beth uffern ti wedi gwneud nawr*?' ('What the hell have you done now?')

For a moment the crowd went silent as the players gathered

around, mystified by the red colouring on my head and face. Clearly everybody thought I had been badly cut as I dived in. Even Gerry Lewis, the Welsh physiotherapist, seemed perturbed as he raced up. 'What have you done, Gareth, what have you done?' Jeff Young, our hooker, soon realized what had happened. He broke into a huge grin as Gerry began wiping away the 'blood' – which was nothing more harmless than the red clay of the Arms Park.

It may seem egotistical, but I savoured the ovation the crowd gave that try. They may have been stunned at the start of the run, but they really let vent as I began to head back towards my own half. No matter how often I see the try on television or read the press cuttings, it was that triumphant walk back which impressed me. I was alone, gathering my thoughts and feeling a glowing sense of achievement – and wanting to know where the hell Dai Morris had been!

The try, without a doubt, was the most satisfying of my career. Luck, vision – and Bill Samuel – had played their part, and Wales went on to win 35–12, which was and still is the biggest championship match score by any side against Scotland. Wales by the end had scored five tries, which was our biggest total against the Scots in Wales.

The only moment of regret in the whole afternoon was seeing iron man J. P. R. Williams go off with a broken jaw. At least it proved he was mortal like the rest of us. Phil Bennett took J.P.R.'s place, which meant the Llanelli Wizard played in four different positions in the first four internationals – fullback, wing, fly half and centre.

Strictly speaking, Phil played in five different positions for Wales. Those with good memories for detail will recall that he took over at scrum half against Australia in 1973 when I had to go off injured near the end, an emergency role before Clive Shell came on as official replacement to earn his one and only cap.

I don't mean to sound ungracious, but I enjoyed playing against Scotland. They are so like the Welsh in many ways. Write them off at your peril! They will defy the odds – and the critics – and as they steam into the first scrum their warcry 'Pundi – pundi – pundi' is enough to rattle any over-confidence you might have.

On tour I have particularly enjoyed the company of the Scots, since a tour allows you time and situations in which to establish friendships. At first they are reserved, even distant, though never stand-offish. Once the ice is broken, however, and you are accepted, their friendship and counsel is genuine and generous. By and large Scottish players come from the executive and professional class, which probably explains why they have an infinite capacity to analyse and debate the game for hours on end. I've spent many hours with 'Mighty Mouse' McLauchlan, not always understanding the profundity of scrummaging and pressure points, but enjoying immensely his deep passion for the niceties of front-row play. Then there is Gordon Brown, always with a smile on his face, a delightful friend and fearsome opponent. I never liked playing against Gordon, but he'd be one of the first I would seek out after a match. There were many others, and from the time an Edinburgh landlord asked me for my ID when I was thirteen and on my first Murrayfield trip to this day, Scotland's 'braves' have had my genuine affection.

With regard to the players against whom I have been directly opposed – the Scottish scrum halves – I have come up against a good variety, from Alex Hastie to Doug Morgan. It would be invidious to single out one of them and describe him as the best, because in an infinite number of ways each player is different and possesses different qualities. I found that Duncan Paterson and Doug Morgan were two excellent players, very competitive and skilled. None of the Scots' scrum halves, in all honesty, presented me with intractable problems, but I gained an enormous respect for Ian McCrae, who was a little terrier, tenacious and game, and who was on top of you all the time. The disciplines of international rugby make it a golden rule to minimize one's own mistakes; McCrae was an opponent who sought at every opportunity to force you into error, putting pressure on you whenever he could. That ability alone made him a very good player.

Wales: J. P. R. Williams; T. G. R. Davies, A. J. Lewis, R. T. E. Bergiers, J. C. Bevan; B. John, G. O. Edwards; D. B. Llewelyn, J. Young, D. J. Lloyd (captain), W. D. Thomas, T. G. Evans, W. D. Morris, J. Taylor, T. M. Davies. Rep: P. Bennett for Williams

Scotland: A. R. Brown; W. C. C. Steele, J. N. M. Frame, J. M. Renwick, A. G. Biggar; C. M. Telfer, D. S. Paterson; J. McLauchlan, R. L. Clark, A. B. Carmichael, I. A. Barnes, G. L. Brown, N. A. MacEwan, R. J. Arneil, P. C. Brown (captain). Rep: L. G. Dick for Biggar

Referee: G. A. Jamieson (Ireland)

# 3 Wales *versus* New Zealand

For a Welshman, the supreme challenge on the field of rugby is against the All Blacks. All internationals are important, but none provoke a greater intensity of passion and fervour than Wales *v.* New Zealand. It has been always so, from the very first meeting between the countries in 1905, until 1980 when the All Blacks won at Cardiff to register their eighth victory in eleven matches. It seems that not one of those eleven historic meetings was without controversy, without argument as to the merit of the victory, or failed to produce fierce debate long after it was played. That is the essence of Wales *v.* All Blacks, battles which are eagerly anticipated by both countries and are fought with unbridled determination by both teams. Victory is always an end in itself, but the gaining of the prize determines that the victors respect and applaud the defeated.

My respect for All Black rugby has been undiluted. Their consistency, their implacable belief in their ability to win and their refusal to acknowledge that the opposition is better have made them the most formidable rugby force the world has known. These qualities, which few countries can hope to match, are inherent, and it takes supreme skill and effort to bring them down. I ought to know – I played for Wales five times against them and was never on the winning side.

Like all Welsh boys, I had been nurtured on the folklore

surrounding New Zealand rugby. Their great sides of 1905 and 1924; their immortal players, like George Nepia and Jack Manchester; and their conquests home and away are inextricably interwoven into the backcloth of Welsh rugby history. That our forefathers beat them a little more regularly than we did propagates the legends, made richer and more awe-inspiring in their telling and retelling.

My first sighting of these giants of world rugby, which I grew up to believe they were, was in 1963 when as an impressionable youth I watched them play Cardiff at the Arms Park. It was inconceivable as I stood with my class-mates of Pontardawe Technical School watching Wilson Whineray's great side that within four years I would be playing against the All Blacks. No such illusions entered my sixteen-year-old head . . . I was remembering at the time the criticism by Bill Samuel of my play for Pontardawe that morning before the Cardiff match when I had scored 17 points against Whitchurch GS. Mr Samuel went to some pains to point out that I had missed two kicks to touch and had given my fly half one particularly wretched pass. That was still in my mind as I saw Cardiff run the All Blacks close before Don Clarke with two massive kicks won the match. This first glimpse of the power of All Black rugby left a lasting impression. I understood for the first time what the whole saga really meant. They had an aura of their own; somehow there was a sense of invincibility about them which, unfortunately, lasted throughout my playing life.

Every Welsh player's ambition is to play at the Arms Park – preferably against New Zealand. That is the ultimate test. My moment came in 1967, a year after the Lions had returned from a tour to New Zealand full of awesome tales of their power and ability. My first task was a psychological one – to convince myself that they were human and fallible and that

I was part of a side which had every chance of bringing the Goliaths to their knees.

I hardly knew what to expect. Were they all going to be rugged, massive 10-foot giants who would trample us underfoot? Would they run us ragged with blistering pace? For a youngster like myself, it seemed a daunting prospect. Still, I assured myself, Wales must have a chance. After all, at the time, we led 3–2 in the series between the countries. So history was on our side, regardless of any self-doubts.

## Wales 6 New Zealand 13, Cardiff Arms Park, 11 November 1967

The Arms Park was very soft and wet after heavy rain, and although Wales had selected a big pack, particularly massive in the front row, there was a feeling that the difficult conditions would favour the All Blacks. It had been a blow that Wales had to take the field without Keith Jarrett, who was injured. His goal kicking, as it happened, was badly missed. Both Paul Wheeler and I fluffed important shots at goal.

Still, although the All Blacks were on balance the better side, there was never a moment in the match when I felt we could not beat them. As it turned out, those missed kicks and a couple of tragic errors gave them the verdict.

Norman Gale, Wales's captain, elected to play against the wind and he seemed to have chosen the right option, because the All Blacks were only marginally secure when they reached half time only 8–0 ahead. Quite frankly, I was surprised that we were still in with a shout. When Barry John reduced the deficit with a dropped goal, my confidence soared. 'We can beat them, we can beat them,' I told myself.

Then tragedy. Fergie McCormick decided to attempt a penalty into the wind from 45 metres. 'What the hell is he taking that for?' I asked myself; it seemed inconceivable that he would get anywhere near the posts. He didn't. But when the kick fell short John Jeffery, who had collected it, calamitously committed himself to a hasty back pass under pressure at the Taff end, and up popped Bill Davis to score, McCormick converting. O tragic fate! Suddenly we were 3–13 adrift and the hapless Jeffery was public enemy No. 1 on the terraces. That he was blamed was unfair. Anyone could have made his mistake. As much to blame was the fact that we had had opportunities to score and did not take them. On reflection, too, McCormick's kick was an excellent tactical ploy – the All Blacks raced after it as if it was a garryowen; we were caught napping.

By now I knew how hard and abrasive the match could be. I didn't have time to be in awe of the All Blacks or players like Tremain, Meads, Lochore and Gray. The pressure was enormous. Once Tremain stepped on my arm, which made me realize how heavy – 16 stone – he was. Neither will I forget being trapped in a ruck, the All Black forwards trampling through in time-honoured fashion. Graham Williams, their flanker, grabbed me and sheltered me with his body as the boots flashed over us. 'Come here, youngster,' Graham said, 'get under me.' In the heat of the moment, it was a magnificent gesture by Graham and probably saved me quite a few bruises, if not worse.

Once, too, I tried a huge up-and-under kick, and in following up I collided heavily with Ian MacRae. He was pretty upset at having his eyebrow split open. But afterwards there were no words of recrimination from him. He accepted it philosophically as a total accident. The incident, though, did one thing for me: it proved the All Blacks were human after all – MacRae actually bled from his injury!

I have to concede that during the match and at the postmortems I realized that the All Blacks were everything I expected them to be. They were not as big or as overwhelming as I had been led to believe, but they were ruthless and dedicated in everything they did; they were hard, fit and fast; and they proved they had this knack of winning, something which they utilized to great effect in future matches with Wales.

I have no doubt that the 1967 and 1969 sides were the best All Black teams I played against. They had perfected the art of rucking, their support play was incredible and they used set-piece possession to inflict too much pressure on us. They also made fewer mistakes than Wales.

Another telling factor was their defence. They were tremendous tacklers and coverers. A case in point was during the Barbarians match at Twickenham, when we led 6–3 going into injury time, only for them to score a match-winning try when Stew Wilson failed to find touch. But in truth the All Blacks won that match because of two fantastic tackles by Fergie McCormick on Gerald Davies and Keri Jones, when both of them looked certain to score.

One last point concerning the All Blacks. Much has been made of their aloofness and their unfriendly attitude. I never once found this to be true. In my day, there was a great camaraderie between the players, which was based largely, I presume, on mutual respect. I got to know many of them very well and established quite a few friendships into the bargain. At the end of the 1967 tour, for instance, many Welsh players went down to Cardiff railway station to bid them farewell before they set off for their final match against the Barbarians at Twickenham.

Things may have changed somewhat today. But what hasn't changed is the All Black attitude to playing. Players come and go, but their traditions and winning attitude are unwavering.

Wales: P. J. Wheeler; S. J. Watkins, W. H. Raybould, I. Hall, K. Jones; B. John, G. O. Edwards; D. Williams, N. R. Gale (captain), B. E. Thomas, M. Wiltshire, W. T. Mainwaring, D. Hughes, J. Taylor, J. Jeffery

New Zealand: W. F. McCormick; W. M. Birtwistle, I. R. MacRae, M. J. Dick, W. L. Davis; E. W. Kirton, C. R. Laidlaw; K. F. Gray, B. E. McLeod, B. L. Muller, S. C. Strahan, C. E. Meads, K. R. Tremain, G. C. Williams, B. J. Lochore (captain)

Referee: M. H. Titcomb (England)

# 4 Great Captains

It has been my particular good fortune that throughout my rugby career I have played with several outstanding team captains, men who by example and leadership often made the difference between victory and defeat. Perception bordering on clairvoyance, unflurried decision-taking when panic was contagious made players like John Dawes and Willie John McBride captains apart. Then there were others, like Gerald Davies, who had the personality and philosophy to undermine firmly entrenched traditions and produce a completely new and refreshing attitude to the game.

When Gerald was appointed captain at Cardiff in 1975, his presence was immediately felt. His ideas as to how the game should and could be played were just what the club needed at that time. The most charitable comment that could be made about Cardiff was that we had been in something of a trough; our game seemed totally forward-oriented. I was kicking a bit – probably too much – and we were concentrating on scrummaging to the detriment of other things. We had, I suppose, lost our way somewhat and the old Cardiff fashion, which meant playing with style and character, had been lost. Gerald helped restore it. Gerald appealed to everyone's better instincts: 'We want to win, but let's do it with style and panache.' It is important to realize that Gerald was a club captain, not just a captain on the field. In advocating a change of direction, he was asking the whole club to support him. This they readily did, and Cardiff began to produce a positive fifteen-man game in which every player was required to play a part. As a wing, of course, Gerald's philosophy was based to a degree on selfishness – he didn't fancy hanging around on the fringes while the forwards and the halfbacks got on with the game! His appointment came after a succession of Cardiff captains from the forwards, and although old ideas understandably die hard, leadership by a back was not resented, particularly after we began to win match after match in exhibition style. It was exhilarating to watch and to participate in, and there is no doubt that Gerald's influence, on and off the field, was an important milestone in the club's development. When he began to score more tries than me, I realized his policy was working!

In the case of Dawes and McBride, the captaincy was different. They were captains of sides, rather than clubs – though there were times when Wales were more like a club than a representative XV.

Without a doubt, Dawes was the most influential Welsh captain I played with. He was very much in contrast with the hell-fire, intimidating approach of some of his predecessors. Quiet, soft-spoken, cool and calculating, Dawes obtained just as good a response from the players as those before him who had planted the *hwyl* in our hearts and placed top priority on our passion and pride.

My respect for what Dawes did for Wales never diminished, even when, as coach, he chose Mervyn Davies as captain of Wales in 1975, a time when I felt my game and attitude had matured sufficiently for me to be ready for the captaincy. When I first played for Wales, captaincy was not that important. But as squad sessions were introduced and match preparation improved, the job became more demanding and more appealing.

As Lions captains, it is impossible to separate Dawes and McBride. They were uncannily similar in their approach and attitude. Both realized that they had at their disposal players who were very mature and experienced, who were there to do a job. Both had the nous to take advantage of advice and counsel from the senior players. It became accepted that Dawes's ability as captain, the man who made the right decisions and called the shots on the field, overshadowed his abilities as a player. In contrast, McBride was established as a great player, and he added to his stature as a captain because of his contributions on the playing front.

I was lucky to have played on two successive Lions tours with captains like Dawes and McBride, men who possessed the right qualifications and the right ingredients to lead sides made up of players from different countries. Both were respected and liked by the players, and it cannot be stressed too much how important that is on a major tour.

If Dawes and McBride were similar in many ways, they were, of course, also different in their approach. Willie John loved to lead from the front, like some First World War officer going over the top with a revolver in his hand. 'Follow me, men!' Dawes in contrast was a field general, the strategist with a perception for the whole, who never panicked and who timed his encouragement with masterful judgement.

Willie John was a magnificent leader of the 1974 Lions in South Africa. But without doubt the success of that tour had its roots in the 1971 tour of New Zealand, coached by Carwyn James and led by Dawes. The nucleus of that side became the hard core of Willie John's party.

If one wanted to put a finger on one decision by Dawes as Lions captain which determined the success of the 1971 tour, it was in the Third Test at Wellington.

## New Zealand 3 Lions 13, Wellington, 31 July 1971

Having won the First Test but lost the Second, we arrived at Wellington with the knowledge that a victory in New Zealand's windy city meant that we could not lose the series. I have rarely been part of a side which exuded more confidence. As the team bus approached Wellington, which lay below us, we started to sing, 'We shall overcome.' The singing wasn't up to Treorchy Male Voice Choir standards, but it put us all in the right frame of mind for the task ahead. We were really bristling when we got off the coach at the ground.

What shaped that confidence? After all, the series was 1–1, and the All Blacks had beaten us 22–11 in the previous match. The answer is simple. In the First Test, at Dunedin, we had got off to a perfect start by winning 9–3. Although that match was something of a nightmare for me because after ten minutes I had suffered a slight hamstring injury, we truly showed our mettle in defence. I was limited to tackling all afternoon, and it was necessary, for the All Blacks threw everything at us. Our defence proved equal to the task and with Barry slotting the goals we gained an important psychological advantage.

The All Blacks, of course, are never more dangerous than when they are beaten, and they stormed back to take the next Test at Christchurch. We learned many lessons from that defeat; above all, we realized we were the better team and had the ability to take the series. We reckoned that the All Blacks had given their best at Christchurch, but we also knew that our potential was greater. I was still not 100 per cent fit, but Sid Going had played well and was one of the architects of their victory, so clearly I had something to prove as well. Dawes and Carwyn James put their heads together to sort

RUGBY PLAYERS' GUIDE TO GOOD EATING.
EAR. Considere
a delicacy in
both hemisphere
NECK. Ed
but contains
nourishm
KNUCKLE Hard to swallow
ELBOW unedible
BREAST of FORWARD Not recommended. Has woolly flavour.

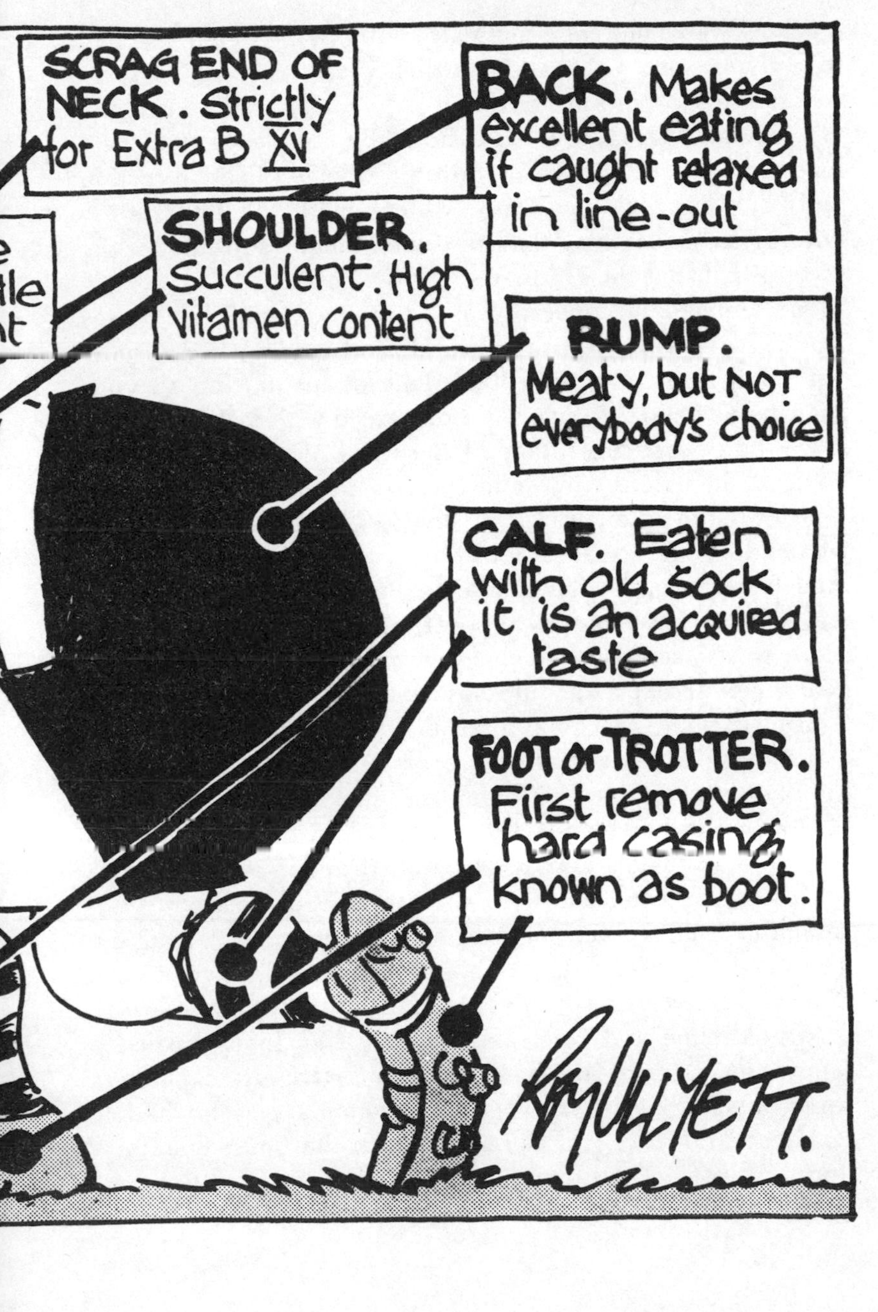

SCRAG END OF NECK. Strictly for Extra B XV
BACK. Makes excellent eating if caught relaxed in line-out
SHOULDER. Succulent. High vitamen content
RUMP. Meaty, but NOT everybody's choice
CALF. Eaten with old sock it is an acquired taste
FOOT or TROTTER. First remove hard casing known as boot.
Roy Ullyett.

out how we would cope tactically with Going. They listened to my views and I agreed with their plan!

Carwyn's attention to detail was underlined when we arrived at Wellington. He immediately rang the local meteorological office to ascertain the velocity, likely direction and duration of the wind which made Wellington so notorious. He learned that the wind might subside by the second half, but the emphasis was on 'might'.

My immediate concern was what decision John Dawes would make if he won the toss. He did, and elected to play with the wind in the first half. Talk about putting all your eggs in one basket! I must say I disagreed with Syd's decision: if we didn't take advantage of the wind in the first half, we could be in serious trouble in the second.

My apprehension was short-lived. The Lions got off to a tremendous start, evidence of our confidence, and we found ourselves scoring 13 points in almost as many minutes. It was a great lead, a psychological boost, but I still thought another score was necessary. Which is why I attempted a dropped goal when perhaps I should have put our line in motion.

Still, 13 points is a good total. Barry had put us ahead with a penalty goal, then Gerald scored a try and finally one of my passes made a try for Barry.

I turned to Barry and said, 'Think of all those listening to the radio at home – Christ, we can't throw it away now.'

Come the second half, and with that good though not uncatchable lead, we went out doggedly determined to hang on. The wind had dropped, which was a great help, and the All Blacks, positively shaken by our first-half performance, were frustrated time and time again. The 1971 Lions earned a reputation for great attacking play. We were also capable of some outstanding defensive work! Even Barry John had to tackle occasionally. Just as important in that tense final forty minutes, we concentrated on not giving away penalties.

Although nothing happened which undermined our confidence that we could last out, it was good to see any sign of discouragement in the All Black camp. It came when Colin Meads, the New Zealand skipper, turned to the referee, Pring, and pleaded in frustation, 'Come on, ref, give us a break.' I knew then that we had them, but even so I felt a little sad watching our forwards totally overwhelm such a player as Brian Lochore. Brian had been brought back into the side as a lock forward, but he was a shadow of his former majestic self and could not cope with the vigorous, determined play of the Lions' locks. It was to prove Brian's final appearance for the All Blacks.

At last, after what seemed an eternity, the final whistle blew. We had won 13–3 and with a 2–1 lead could not now lose the series.

The victory gave us plenty of reason for celebration, but it was specially satisfying for the Welsh contingent who had been part of the humiliation of 1969. Those of us on that trip vowed that, one day, we would make up for that galling experience. That day was at Wellington in July 1971.

The 1971 Lions were very fortunate to have several key players like Mike Gibson and Barry John, but the measurable strength of the side was that it possessed so many varied attacking qualities. The forwards were magnificent too. They gave everything to get us the possession, and they knew that, provided they wrung out, say, 40 per cent possession, we had the backs to score. Even when one player was snuffed out, there were others capable of pulling off a crucial score.

Then there was Dawes's leadership. As I have intimated, his decision to play with the wind proved vital. It was a bold, calculated move, and it not only paid off, but proved his quality as a captain, unafraid to make a decision which some of us thought was wrong at the time!

The record books show that the All Blacks drew the final

Test, which meant that the Lions won the series. It wasn't until we all returned, in triumph, to the UK that the full realization of our achievement dawned on us. Our welcome home was fantastic. There were thousands at Heathrow, and by the time I had got to Neath people were six deep on the roadside as I drove back to Gwaun-cae-Gurwen. Suddenly, it seemed, rugby had become the people's game. The celebrations in the UK went on for months, with parties, dinners and receptions the like of which we players had never before experienced. It was fantastic. And it took me in all nearly nine months fully to get over the 1971 Lions tour of New Zealand.

New Zealand: L. W. Mains; K. R. Carrington, W. D. Cottrell, H. T. Joseph, B. A. Hunter; R. E. Burgess, S. M. Going; B. L. Muller, R. W. Norton, R. A. Guy, C. E. Meads (captain), B. J. Lochore, I. A. Kirkpatrick, A. M. McNaughton, A. J. Wyllie. Rep: M. G. Duncan for Burgess

Lions: J. P. R. Williams; T. G. R. Davies, S. J. Dawes (captain), C. M. H. Gibson, D. J. Duckham; B. John, G. O. Edwards; J. McLauchlan, J. V. Pullin, J. F. Lynch, W. J. McBride, G. L. Brown, J. F. Slattery, J. Taylor, T. M. Davies

Referee: J. P. G. Pring (New Zealand)

# 5 Scrum Halves

As the years since my retirement roll by, one of the most common questions put to me has been: Who was the best scrum half I played against? Considering the number of times this old chestnut comes up, I suppose I should have a pat answer ready, or at least one that would satisfy even the most inquisitive. The truth is there is no answer to the question, certainly not one that would bear scrutiny.

What is not readily understood is that so many factors are required to determine the answer. Scrum halves come in all shapes and sizes: some are tall and wiry, others are short and stocky, some are sharp, essentially attacking players and others are rugged, defensive types. There are those who play well behind a winning pack; others who cope admirably when their forwards are taking a beating. Some pass long; others fire short and bulletlike. Some can kick and run; others never. The types are endless and their skills so varied that it is a futile and unrewarding exercise to discriminate and select one as the best.

What is certain is that an international scrum half is rarely of poor standard. Against some you come off the field absolutely shattered, physically and mentally. Against others, you hardly know they've been playing. So much depends on which side has gained the ascendancy and how well or badly the scrum half copes with the varied situations.

What I can say is that the scrum half who gave me most trouble was Sid Going, of New Zealand. That's hardly surprising since I played against him thirteen times, confrontations which allowed ample opportunity for each of us to get to know the other's qualities and failings. Sid was such a tenacious player that he was always difficult to play against. He was very competitive and aggressive on the field, but off it he was a gentleman, quiet and unassuming. I played against him more than against any other scrum half, yet paradoxically never got to know him. We never developed a friendship or rapport. There is no such thing as a poor New Zealand scrum half at any level – their type of play demands and breeds highly skilled scrum halves – this was certainly the case with Chris Laidlaw, whom I played against in 1967. I was a young, inexperienced player then and impressionable enough to form a lasting regard for Laidlaw and probably the best All Black side ever. Chris and Sid were so different in their play. Chris had much more variety and, of course, he possessed a superb pass which was long, accurate, smooth, one flowing blurr. In contrast Sid's pass was a hiccup and a spit, but few played better in close attendance with an All Black pack when it was in command and driving forward. Like many others, however, Going was noticeably less effective when his forwards were not on top.

All the French scrum halves I came up against had one thing in common – they were quick and razor-sharp. The French, though, rarely maintained faith with one scrum half for long – at least in my time – and I often found myself in a one-off confrontation. It is, therefore, impossible to make a valid judgement concerning French scrum halves, with the possible exception of Lilian Camberabero, who stood out from the rest because of his huge pass. None of the French, in all honesty, gave me any serious bother as competitors. Generally, whoever I played against I managed to keep under lock and key.

The Irish had some very good scrum halves, from Roger Young, to John Moloney and John Robbie. Roger was an orthodox, straightforward player, but he was very strong and had the important attribute of making few mistakes under pressure. I struck up a very close friendship with Roger, who now has a successful dentistry practice in Cape Town. He writes to me regularly, at least once a week. He complains I do not write back. We have compromised. He writes, I phone.

Jan Webster, of England, was probably the bravest scrum half I ever played against. Jan took a lot of hammerings and deserved greater recognition for his gutsy play. Another Englishman, Steve Smith, was something of an enigma. Potentially he was very good; he had all the attributes, and confidence and ability, to succeed. Somehow, Steve just failed to gain a place in the higher echelons. He lacked some ingredient. Credit though to him that, after being dropped, he grasped the second opportunity. I feel, however that his was an untapped talent.

I was a distant admirer of Australia's inimitable Ken Catchpole, and I regret I never had the opportunity of playing against him. In fact, I played only against John Hipwell in the three internationals I played against Australia, although I must also include Rod Hauser who came on as a replacement for Hipwell in the 1975 Wales *v.* Australia match. Hipwell was a sturdy, powerful scrum half, but he rarely caught you unawares in anything he attempted.

I came up against Dawie de Villiers three times in South Africa and three times in the UK, and I had great respect for him, both on and off the field. He was a good tactical player, neat, tidy and undeniably tougher than his cherubic looks suggested. He gave the Lions a lot of problems in 1968 when he varied his tactics excellently. Another who might have been cast in the de Villiers mould was Roy McCallum, the leading candidate for the Springbok team in 1974, but who only managed to play one Test, the crucial first one, because of injury. Bayvel and Sonnekus, his successors, hardly sent a ripple of alarm through the Lions ranks, but once again criticism of them has to be tempered by the fact that they were playing behind a beaten pack.

The Lions of 1974 were, of course, described as the greatest. Not only did they march through South Africa unbeaten, but they shattered all sorts of records en route. It was something very special to be part of that legendary tour, on which, as in New Zealand in 1971, the Lions shrugged off criticism and became one of the most successful touring sides in the history of the game. The crucial encounter, as on all tours, came in the First Test at Cape Town. Winning that primed us to take the series, which we did. Even a draw in the last Test took none of the shine off that sparkling tour.

## South Africa 3 Lions 12, Newlands, Cape Town, 8 June 1974

Newlands was wet and sticky after rain when the 1974 Lions came to Cape Town to prove that victories in their first seven provincial matches were no fluke. Incomprehensibly, the South African authorities allowed two curtain-raisers to be played on the Test pitch, which was churned up unnecessarily. The conditions dictated the type of game we would play.

Personally, I was sceptical of success in this First Test; I recalled what had happened on the previous tour, in 1968, when we had also won all our pre-First Test matches and then come unstuck at Pretoria. The chief difference, which proved crucial, was that this 1974 side was much more experienced and mature. We had already built a collective will to win which by the end of the tour was quite irrepressible.

The Springboks, on the other hand, were snatching at straws in their selection. They had completely misinterpreted our below-par performance against Western Province, which was nothing more than a hiccup in our preparation and planning. We had won that match 17–8 after a struggle, but we all knew we were infinitely better than the result indicated. Naturally, we were positively delighted when the Springbok selectors chose eight of the Western Province side to play in the Test. We also made a significant change to the pencilled-in Test team – Mervyn Davies got the nod ahead of Andy Ripley.

Still, the South Africans are masters at psychological intimidation. Their newspapers were full of photographs of their mighty pack, featuring particularly a massive front row. The Lions were going to have their heads chewed off! The only people who seemed to be relishing the challenge – I must say I was apprehensive, to say the least – were our front row. Mighty Mouse, Bobby Windsor and Fran Cotton could hardly wait to get to grips with those South African giants.

Predictably, in horrible conditions, the battle of the front row was the key to the outcome. There was tremendous pride at stake as well, for it must be remembered that the Springboks had built their traditions on their scrummaging ability. What a battle it was, up front, at least until the second half. If I needed a confidence booster, it came when one scrum broke up and the referee, Max Baise, ordered the packs to go down again. Clearly, those big Boks simply didn't fancy it. Van Wyk stood off and Windsor said, 'Come here, you pudding face. . .' Cotton had to reach out and drag his opponent into the scrum. That reluctance, indeed diffidence, confirmed to me that we – or at least our front-row union – had scored a most important psychological victory. If you beat the Springboks in the scrum, you can beat them elsewhere.

So it proved. The longer the match progressed, the more emphatic was our forward domination. Towards the end, even though we were never very far in front, and then only because of three Phil Bennett penalties and a dropped goal from myself, my confidence surged. The Lions ran out winners, but, more important, it gave us that crucial edge. We all knew then that, apart from some miraculous intervention on behalf of the Springboks, we would win the series. It was a tremendous feeling, a mixture of elation and anticipation.

On the team bus travelling to the ground I had opened a letter from home. It contained a picture of my son, Owen, who was only a few days old when I left on tour. I was so chuffed that I decided there and then to go out and play my heart out, just for him. But I didn't tell Mighty Mouse, Bobby or Fran that!

Self-praise for the 1974 Lions was, by the end, unnecessary. Everyone did that for us. Even the South Africans paid high tributes, although being beaten must have been somewhat galling for them in view of their long and spectacular run of triumphs against allcomers to the High Veldt. The best summing-up of that tour, in fact, came from one of the greatest of all Springbok threequarters, John Gainsford: '[The Lions] were mentally tougher, physically harder, superbly drilled and coached and disciplined and united. They were dedicated fellows who were trained to peak fitness, who were prepared like professionals and who were ready to die on the field for victory.'

South Africa: I. McCallum; G. Muller, P. Whipp, J. Oosthuzen, A. Read; D. Snyman, R. McCallum; J.

Prince Charles, on his first public engagement as the Prince of Wales, is introduced to the Welsh players by Brian Price before the match against Ireland at Cardiff Arms Park on 8 March 1969

Big Brian Thomas, battered and bandaged Welsh hero of the controversial match against Ireland in 1969. Brian's return to the fray after injury swung the match in Wales's favour

Noel Murphy, arm lifted protectively, falls victim of Brian Price's retaliation

A moment of decision for Phil Bennett, the wizard from Llanelli, against England at the Arms Park in 1973

The sight that must have terrified the opposition – my old pal and Cardiff club-mate, Gerald Davies, in full cry

Life was very simple for a scrum half when Barry John, uncannily gifted in taking all sorts of passes, was your partner at fly-half

J.P.R. Williams, so often the last line of Wales's defence – rocklike, fearless but always prepared to counter-attack

Keith Jarrett, the fresh-faced schoolboy, who tore England and the record book to shreds on his debut in 1967

Mervyn Davies, master of all he surveyed at the tail of the Welsh line-out, against France in 1972

Another try for J.J. Williams, one of three that he scored which helped Wales to beat Australia by a record margin of 28–3 at Cardiff in 1975

John Dawes, who played an important part in the famous Barbarians try against the All Blacks in 1973 – all the work was done before I came up to finish it off!

'Dai' Duckham, an old adversary, but who was one of the most popular England players in Wales because of his attacking flair

Fergus Slattery, the Irish fireball, putting some pressure on Barry John. 'Slatts' was a very good, highly committed player

Jérôme Gallion, the French scrum half, whose challenge added spice to my final match for Wales, at Cardiff on 18 March 1978

Frik du Preez, the formidable South African forward, is inconvenienced by a little leg-pulling from a Cardiff scrum half, in 1970

Sid Going, the All Blacks scrum half, was the player who gave me most trouble during my career. We played against each other thirteen times

The length and quality of my passing was often the subject of much debate during my career: suffice to say I believe it was better at the end of my playing days than at the beginning

The bravest scrum half I ever played against was England's Jan Webster, a gritty, gutsy little character if ever there was one

Willie John McBride on a high after he had captained the British Lions to a series-clinching victory over South Africa at Port Elizabeth in 1974

The Lions forwards on the rampage – 'Mighty Mouse' McLauchlan leads the charge against Northern Transvaal during our fabulous unbeaten 1974 tour of South Africa

The French forwards have clobbered me here, but fortunately I got my pass in for Phil Bennett to score one of his two tries in 1978

They say you always remember the first one – well, my last try for Wales, against Scotland on 18 February 1978, was no less satisfying

Sauerman, J. Van Wyk, J. H. F. Marais (captain), J. Williams, K. de Klerk, J. Coetzee, J. Ellis, M. du Plessis

Lions: J. P. R. Williams; J. J. Williams, R. A. Milliken, I. R. McGeechan, W. C. C. Steele; P. Bennett, G. O. Edwards; I. McLauchlan, R. W. Windsor, F. E. Cotton, G. L. Brown, W. J. McBride (captain), R. M. Uttley, J. F. Slattery, T. M. Davies

Referee: M. Baise (South Africa)

# 6 Millfield

## Llanelli GS 3 Millfield 5, Stradey Park, Llanelli, 1964

When I first went to Millfield, in 1964, I have to admit I didn't really know much about the place. That, in the readily misunderstood world of public schools, it was an exception I had yet to realize. My enthusiasm for the school was really fired only when I was told that one of the pupils there was the magnificent athlete, Mary Bignal. The man who arranged for me to become a boarder was Bill Samuel, my mentor and friend, who for some time had looked at the prospect of my being taught there for one reason only – it was an opportunity of a lifetime to grow up and mature in a school where the pursuit of excellence at sport was fundamental.

Only years later did I fully appreciate what Millfield did for me, in terms of widening my vision and sharpening my appreciation of life as a whole. In athletic terms, Millfield was superb, with a range of facilities and opportunities the envy of other academic nurseries.

Millfield was also different from many other public schools in that the pupils came from every walk of life. It was totally cosmopolitan with pupils from all over the world. Its success can be measured in that many who were taught there have since gone on to become diplomats, missionaries, politicians

. . . and quite a few have become household names in the world of sport.

Although I succeeded in obtaining a place at Millfield primarily as the result of my ability as an athlete, it wasn't long before rugby became my main preoccupation. Millfield's reputation as a rugby school was due entirely to the headmaster, 'Boss' Meyer, who was a rugby fanatic, and his wife, Joyce. Schools which originally had been willing only to play their Second XVs against Millfield, suddenly found their First XVs overwhelmed. Although Millfield had a wide range of sporting activities for the pupils, as at Oxford and Cambridge the most compelling athletic activity revolved around rugby.

Matches became very important events, so much so that on one occasion I decided to play for Millfield in the Roehampton Schools Sevens rather than gain a Welsh Schoolboy cap. Preparation for more serious rugby came in the shape of matches against, for instance, the Colts of Racing Club de Paris, the Somerset Barbarians and a multitude of invitation XVs, which often contained some of the best players in Britain.

We weren't all Welsh in the Millfield First XV. We had, in 1963 for instance, players from Argentina, Brazil, Colombia, Siam and Ireland.

Millfield's esprit de corps became famous, and we took on and usually beat some of the best school sides in the land. Once the *Daily Telegraph* began reporting our progress, we knew we had arrived! So, in 1964, a match was arranged against Llanelli Grammar School which, like ourselves, had made the schools column of the *Telegraph* and were enjoying a very good season. It seemed the most natural challenge match of the time. And no one knew better than I that it would also be the schoolboy test of a lifetime.

The other Millfield players understood the importance of a match against Llanelli, but with my Welsh background I could imagine all those unofficial Big Five selectors on the 'Tanner Bank' at Llanelli looking on and assessing who would go on to become Scarlets – and Welsh players – in the future. I also knew that few countries matched the intensity of Welsh schoolboy rugby. Llanelli themselves had been accused of 'professionalism' because of the way they prepared and practised for the Roehampton Schools Sevens. Their only crime, though, was that they won the title far too often. Jealousy and prejudice breeds just as profusely at public schools as it does anywhere else.

Llanelli had a tremendous record that season, probably the best in Britain. Clearly it was going to be a great test for Millfield, and a fine opportunity to establish the school in the forefront of school rugby academies. I'm not sure that we all felt that, but the anticipation for the match with Llanelli was tremendous. Talk about adrenalin. I think I'd have popped if someone had stuck a pin in me just before the match. The great event took place at Stradey Park, Llanelli's club ground, simply because of the fantastic interest the challenge had created. Imagine my feelings, not only eager to prove myself, but at one of Wales's most famous rugby grounds and, inevitably, in front of my father and mother, plus a few aunts and uncles, some of whom needed pretty convincing evidence that I was not wasting my time in that posh school in England.

The train journey from Somerset to Llanelli was exhilarating. It was raining and miserable as we entered the Severn Tunnel, but, like some divine omen, the sun burst out as we reappeared in Wales. (I didn't dare tell the rest of the Millfield lads that weatherwise it was usually the reverse!) We had some interesting players, to say the least. There was Varni Dennis, 6 feet 1 inch from Liberia and an even-timer over 100 yards; Louis Bush, son of a Brazilian millionaire, who was to become a missionary in El Salvador; and Vaughan Williams, already capped for Welsh Secondary Schools. I hoped that they wouldn't let me down. For my part, I was determined they would have no similar grounds for worry.

Llanelli RFC had played Richmond at Stradey in the afternoon, a senior club match which had attracted a couple of thousand or so. By the time the floodlights were switched on for our match, the number of spectators had swollen. There must have been 6000 present when Britain's two major unbeaten schools kicked off on a cool, drizzly evening.

Apart from some vociferous shouts from the folk of Gwauncae-Gurwen, it was quite obvious there were many present shouting for Millfield. Bill Samuel, naturally, was there. He wanted to see if he had been right about arranging for me to go to the school.

With both sides full of talented, eager players, it was a marvellous exhibition of fluent, open rugby. Years afterwards, some who watched it come up to me and ask, 'Do you remember that match between Llanelli GS and Millfield?' As if I could forget it!

From all the running, the thrusts and counterthrusts, the score could have been 55–33. It was in fact 5–3 to Millfield, a scoreline that disguised some of the most enjoyable, exciting and uninhibited rugby I've been part of. It was not all running. The tackling was furious, bruising. The commitment of both sides was incredible. If Millfield took the ball, say, 30 metres, a tackle would deprive us of possession and Llanelli would tear away, and they were only stopped by some last-ditch desperate defence. I recall trying to cut away on the blind side, only to find three, or maybe it was four, red-, green-, and white-hooped Llanelli players poised waiting to engulf me.

A few minutes from the end Llanelli worked the ball clear for their wing, Lyndon Jones. Lyndon surged to the line and it looked as if Millfield's winning grip would be prised from us. I gave chase and with a desperate lunge I managed to bring Lyndon down short of the line. Schoolgirl supporters of Llanelli shrieked their disappointment. I felt a bit like Roy of the Rovers, having saved the match for my side in a desperate finish! The pride, the thrill of it all and the exhaustion were for later.

If this reminiscence smacks a little of the sentimentality of an overgrown schoolboy, I'm sorry. It was my first experience of a 'big match', and because it was a marvellous contest, open and free, and full of so much commitment, it remains very high on my list of best-remembered matches.

# 7 Wales *versus* Ireland

Of all the countries I have played against for Wales, none seems to have given us consistently more trouble than Ireland. There were occasions when they did not fulfil the expectations of their supporters, but generally the Irish played out of their skins against the Welsh, particularly at Lansdowne Road. It is difficult to imagine a country playing with more pride and passion than Ireland! They would pitch into you with such ferocity you'd think their lives were at stake.

For guys who love 'the crack', who were happy-go-lucky off the field, this transformation was amazing. Unfortunately for the Irish, their playing with their hearts and not their heads cost them dearly in many matches, and not only against Wales. We used to have a saying that the Irish had but one tactic: 'Kick ahead – any bloody head.' There was no doubt, however, that Ireland played a simple, forward-oriented game, in which aggression, uncompromising or otherwise, provided the opposition with some searching examinations. They were spoilers to a man, and even if they could not produce sustained quality play, they made absolutely certain that their opposition couldn't either. This is not a criticism, more an observation, for generally Irish teams, particularly their forwards, played the basics of the game very well indeed.

It is curious that with this tradition for forward play the Irish should have produced over the years so many exceptional backs, such as the peerless Mike Gibson, Barry McGann, Tony Ward and Tom Grace, players of my era but representative of a heritage of talented players. I have a theory about this Irish production line. A lot of Irish children are nurtured on two highly skilful games, hurling and Gaelic football – not to mention soccer – and much of what they have learned rubs off when they transfer to rugby football. They simply adapt the skills they have already learned. Yet despite the brilliance of some of the Irish backs, more significant on the day was the fact that Ireland as a team were always so difficult to beat. When Wales did defeat them, it was only after we had swum against the tide for a very long time.

I played ten championship matches against Ireland and I've not forgotten any of them. But the ones that stand out in sharp relief were the first two, mostly because of the controversy they contained, and my final match against Ireland in 1978, that fantastic year when Wales won the Triple Crown for the third season in a row.

## Ireland 9 Wales 6, Lansdowne Road, Dublin, 9 March 1968

This was my fifth championship match but the first time I had played against the Irish, indeed the first time I had been to Ireland, let alone played at the oldest of all the international stadiums, Lansdowne Road. I was never to forget the occasion, largely because the referee, England's Mike Titcomb, decided that a drop kick I had attempted had gone inside the posts when everyone thought the kick had missed. What a kerfuffle that kick caused, although it did not materially affect the result because Ireland won with a try by Mick Doyle in injury time.

It was an odd occasion all round for me for, having captained Wales in our previous match against Scotland, I was relieved of the leadership against Ireland. The selectors decided the Welsh cause would be better served with John Dawes as skipper. In my opinion, Dawes didn't do anything wrong at Lansdowne Road, either as a player or captain, but he too lost the captaincy for the next match, against France at Cardiff. I resumed the duties when the cockahoop French won the Grand Slam for the first time.

But back to that famous, or should it be infamous, dropped goal. The Irish, particularly their pack, were subjecting Wales to a great deal of pressure, and it took all our best efforts to keep them at bay. It must have been a fascinating experience for my Cardiff club-mate, Maurice Richards, who was receiving his first cap. Because we weren't winning too much ball he spent most of the match surveying the scene from the left wing. This certainly wasn't the occasion for Maurice to show off his blistering pace and try-getting qualities.

Even the most ardent of Welsh supporters would have hardly complained that Ireland did not deserve to be 6–3 ahead, thanks to a penalty goal by their captain, Tom Kiernan, and a dropped goal by Mike Gibson, on this occasion playing at outside half. There was, incidentally, some doubt too about Gibbo's dropped goal – several Welsh players claimed it should not have been allowed because the ball had been touched in flight, an act which disqualified a dropped goal in those days. John Taylor was adamant that it was he who got a hand to the ball after Gibson had kicked, and knowing Bas as I do, I believe his claim implicitly.

Arguments apart, the Irish *were* ahead and something needed to be done about it. In that kind of desperate and tense situation, any score would suffice – even the most unlikely, such as a dropped goal from yours truly.

Of all the things I have attempted on the field of rugby,

and some have been bizarrely unexpected, none was more so than this. It was, essentially, an act of spontaneity, a spur-of-the-moment decision, with as much hope of success as bringing down a fly with a peashooter.

We had driven forward to within striking distance of the Irish line when the chance came. At once I was given the opportunity of getting Barry away with a pass, or even Dai Morris, who was hovering. But as I wound the pass up, I noticed out of the corner of my eye that the Irish cover had swept across, and that both Barry and Dai were likely to be stifled as soon as either of them got the ball. So, with the ball almost leaving my hands, I pulled the pass back at the last moment, changed direction in a flash, and hit a real purler from about 30 metres. There was a strong, swirling wind, and as the kick soared high, dead centre, at the last moment the wind caught it and sent it over one of the posts. Nevertheless, it was close enough to have carried inside the post and I actually threw my hands in the air and cried out exultantly, 'It's there, it's there.'

The referee, meanwhile, had been caught out by my quick change of direction. He had been setting off to follow the expected pass to Barry or Dai and, when I changed my mind, he had to twist around while still running. It was this probably more than anything else that limited his sight of the kick, and I suppose that, when I loudly shouted that the kick had gone home, Mr Titcomb might have been influenced had he been in any doubt. After all, rugby players don't generally claim a score unless they are reasonably certain it is valid!

A lot of people have suggested that the referee was a victim of a con trick and that I was guilty of an indecent act of gamesmanship. That was certainly not true. I took the kick quickly and instinctively – and I genuinely thought the goal had been scored. The only doubt came moments later, when the Irish fans went wild.

The scenes were extraordinary. Not only did some of the irate fans rush on the pitch, but others underlined their disagreement with Mr Titcomb's decision by throwing missiles. I began to have my doubts about the kick when a Guinness bottle – presumably empty – whizzed a couple of inches past my head. When coins and other missiles showered on, I was fairly convinced that Mr Titcomb had made a mistake and that the kick had not gone over! The Irish team were heroic in helping to calm things down. We Welsh players were certainly grateful for that; probably so was the referee, by now very shaken and white-faced. Later, and this speaks highly of him, he conceded that he might have erred.

Had we hung on or even scored a match-winner, I have no doubt we'd have had a riot on our hands at Lansdowne Road. As it was, Mick Doyle's try gave Ireland the victory, a result which restored the humour and satisfaction in the stands. Mr Titcomb didn't really require the police escort from the ground when he blew for full time.

Ireland: T. J. Kiernan (captain) A. T. A. Duggan, L. Hunter, F. P. K., Bresnihan, J. C. M. Moroney; C. M. H. Gibson, R. M. Young; P. O'Callaghan, A. M. Brady, S. Millar, W. J. McBride, M. G. Molloy, M. G. Doyle, T. J. Doyle, K. G. Goodall

Wales: D. Rees; W. K. Jones, S. J. Dawes (captain), W. H. Raybould, M. C. R. Richards; B. John, G. O. Edwards, J. P. O'Shea, J. Young, D. J. Lloyd, I. C. Jones, W. D. Thomas, W. D. Morris, J. Taylor, R. E. Jones

Referee: M. H. Titcomb (England)

## Wales 24 Ireland 11, Cardiff Arms Park, 8 March 1969

J. P. R. Williams and Mervyn Davies, who had made their debuts for Wales at Murrayfield a month previously, made their first international appearances at Cardiff Arms Park, where stand rebuilding limited the attendance to 29,000, plus the Prince of Wales.

The pundits had forecast a searching examination for all of us. Ireland, basking in the glory of six championship matches without defeat, had come to Wales in search of the Grand Slam, a prize which had eluded them for twenty-one years.

The match, predictably, was full of incident and controversy, most of it emanating from the so-called Murphy Plan. Although my Irish friends may doubt it, there was in fact no such thing as the Murphy Plan, which was purported to be some heinous Welsh plot to draw the teeth of that tiger of Irish forwards, Noel Murphy.

Despite being injured in the victory over France, Noel had played an inspiring part in Ireland's subsequent wins against England and Scotland and, rightly, was highly regarded as a motivator. If we had any notion to diminish Noel's contribution it was simply to dampen his enthusiasm somewhat by rucking him New Zealand fashion early in the match. It was more an idea, rather than any insidious plot, and it required that I secure the ball from the first scrum, drive into Murphy and then our forwards would drive over both of us. The New Zealanders had used similar ploys for years and there was certainly nothing underhand about it, particularly as it was agreed it should be performed under the referee's nose. But, as they say, the best plans of mice and men can be undone – in this case by a mole in the Welsh camp who, a day before the match, revealed all to the Irish. 'Look out for the Murphy Plan,' they were warned.

Forewarned doesn't necessarily mean forearmed, however, for within three minutes Murphy was very much the centre of events. He was floored by a punch from Brian Price, the Welsh captain, who, if his opposite number, Tom Kiernan, had prevailed in his protestations, would have been sent off for the offence. From way back at fullback Tom began shouting, 'It's the Murphy Plan, ref. It's the bloody Murphy Plan. Send him off.' Fortunately, Mr McMahon, recognizing an element of severe provocation, turned a deaf ear to Tom's request, and although the Irish complained bitterly among themselves about the incident for a while they soon got on with the game.

Meanwhile Wales had their own problems. For the first twenty minutes I didn't even put the ball into a scrum. And, on top of that, the Irish put us under so much pressure, and kicked two penalties, that there was no chance to execute the so-called Murphy Plan.

About half an hour later, the match erupted yet again when Ireland's hooker, Ken Kennedy, was floored by another punch. This time there was no holding the outraged Kiernan. It didn't help that no one, including myself, knew what had happened. I am since of the opinion that there was an element of truth in Denzil Williams's explanation: that the punch concerned had been thrown by one of the Irish second row, that it was intended for Denzil's angelic features but had missed and Ken inopportunely put his face in the way. For a while the Irish fury nearly boiled over and their passion looked uncontrollable. All hell seemed set to break loose and, if I hadn't been so concerned with the consequences, I honestly believe I would have been laughing my head off. It was not a case of funny ha-ha, but funny peculiar.

Tom Kiernan was still beside himself with anger and wouldn't listen to our explanations or protests – and in my view, this failure and refusal by the Irish team to settle down and capitalize on their 6–3 lead cost them the match. Their discipline disappeared, they allowed the incidents to determine their attitude and actions and quite simply lost the Grand Slam because they lost their rag.

By this time the action had reached fever pitch. It seemed all set to explode once more when Brian Thomas was stamped on by an Irish forward. A deep gash was opened up and our hearts sank when we realized that big Brian would have to go off. His importance to our forward effort could not be overemphasized – the strong man of the scrum, the rock whom no one could remember having to leave the field before. Although this was the first season when substitutes were allowed, the loss of Thomas was a huge psychological blow. It was to the Welsh team's credit, however, that we refused to allow the incident to dishearten us completely. In fact, we resolved to put in even more effort, and we were doing just that, pushing forward to win a scrum into the Irish 25, when there was a tremendous roar from the crowd. Thomas, head stitched and bandaged, had reappeared on the touch-line ready to resume duty.

What a tonic his reappearance was for Wales. His return signalled the beginning of the end of Irish hopes. He at once slotted back into the pack, and such was his strength and drive that the scrum moved forward nearly 3 metres. What a shove! What a man! From then on, there was going to be only one possible outcome. Ireland, if not taken apart, were outplayed and we gained a complete victory. The Murphy Plan? We didn't need it.

I have been asked many times about the Brian Price incident. I am happy to accept his explanation, that he reacted to being clawed about the face and that he had spontaneously 'let one fly'. That Noel Murphy was the recipient of the punch probably was accidental, and in no way suggests that he was in fact the clawing culprit. In the event,

Doug McMahon, the referee, recognized that some injustice would be deemed to have been done if he sent off Price. The referee even went so far as to admit that he had handled far rougher matches. As for Noel Murphy, he did not play for Ireland again. He was a tremendous competitor on the field and, regardless of the incidents in this match, he was highly thought of by friend and foe. In other words, a good player.

Wales: J. P. R. Williams; S. J. Watkins, K. S. Jarrett, T. G. R. Davies, M. C. R. Richards; B. John, G. O. Edwards; D. Williams, J. Young, D. J. Lloyd, B. Price (captain), B. E Thomas, W. D. Morris, J. Taylor, T. M. Davies

Ireland: T. J. Kiernan (captain); A. T. A. Duggan, F. P. K. Bresnihan, C. M. H. Gibson, J. C. M. Moroney; B. J. McGann, R. M. Young; P. O'Callaghan, K. W. Kennedy, S. Millar, W. J. McBride, M. G. Molloy, J. C. Davidson, N. A. A. Murphy, M. L. Hipwell

Referee: D. C. J. McMahon (Scotland)

## Ireland 16 Wales 20, Lansdowne Road, Dublin, 4 March 1978

It is a matter of fact if not regret that several Wales–Ireland clashes have been marred by unsavoury incidents. I remember this one particularly well, not only because it marked the end of Gerald Davies's magnificent championship career and my own last appearance against Ireland, but because my old pal, Fergus Slattery, lost his cool.

The occasion should have been one of celebration for Ireland, if only because Mike Gibson was making a world record sixty-fourth appearance. It turned out to be the hardest match physically I have ever played in. And I dare say that might go for a lot of the Welsh players, many of whom an hour after the match were still slumped on the changing-room benches, too whacked to draw breath, let alone change.

It was a match which more or less made up my mind that I should retire. Enough was enough. As I sat in the changing room, worn out like everyone else, I knew I was never again going back to Lansdowne Road. There was no champagne to celebrate our Triple Crown victory, no elation. Nothing except the conviction that I'd given everything and there was no more to give. Cliff Jones, chairman of the selectors, tried to buck us all up. He kept telling us what a great victory it had been, how well we had done, how rare it was to win the Triple Crown. We all stared at him and said nothing.

Even later, after the match banquet, everyone was still subdued. Stan Thomas, of Cardiff, invited some of us to a late party at Dun Laoghaire. I refused politely. I told Stan I simply didn't feel like it. In fact I was drained both mentally and physically. It was almost as if we had lost by 30 points.

The match itself was curious. Wales, eager to win the Triple Crown, suddenly found themselves incredibly 11–0 ahead.

'I don't like this,' Gerald Davies said to me. 'I don't like it at all, it's far too easy.'

'I agree with you, Ger,' I replied.

Whatever our worst fears were at that moment, they were soon to be realized in the shape of a furious onslaught from Ireland. It was not so much a comeback as an avalanche as they poured in on us, bombarding us with garryowens and surging after them like men demented.

The referee, Georges Domercq, meanwhile was allowing far too loose a match. He let almost everything go, and in that mad, hysterical scramble there was a lot that was clearly against the law. There was one blatant Irish knock-on and the French referee, waving his hands forward, told everyone to 'keep it going'. It was an attitude ideal in charity matches, but wrong at Lansdowne Road.

It didn't help matters either when J.P.R. bodychecked Mike Gibson. The crowd went wild. But more important, the Irish players were furious, translating their anger into even greater physical effort. I cannot remember a match in which Wales were under greater pressure. We were against the ropes and taking a real pounding. On one occasion I let one go at Moss Keane as he trampled through a ruck. It was like a fly swatting an elephant. Domercq penalized me for it. In view of what was going on all around, it was a laughable decision.

The Irish plainly had decided to take no prisoners and, regardless of the means, the end seemed to be justified, for they pulled back from that big early deficit to level at 16–16.

There was about five minutes left when I told the pack to forget their weariness, their cuts and bruises. 'Come on, let's have one last effort.' One moment they were exhausted, almost beaten, the next they found that extra bit of effort for which I had pleaded. As a scrum went down, first Bobby Windsor drove in, then Wheelo, then the back row and whoomph, just like a shunting engine, we powered towards the Irish line. The ball came back to me, and I could only give a scrappy pass to Benny. He served Fenwick, who put in an overhead pass to J.J., and the Llanelli wing flew in for the try. We had won! The recriminations came later. Our consolation was that that was what winning a Triple Crown was all about. To be honest, winning was the only satisfaction in one of the roughest, most demanding matches of my career.

Ireland: A. H. Ensor; C. M. H. Gibson, A. R. McKibbin, P. P. McNaughton, A. C. McLennan; A. J. P. Ward, J. J. Moloney (captain); E. M. J. Byrne, P. C. Whelan, P. A. Orr,

M. J. Keane, H. W. Steele, S. A. McKinney, J. F. Slattery, W. P. Duggan

Wales: J. P. R. Williams; T. G. R. Davies, R. W. R. Gravell, S. P. Fenwick, J. J. Williams; P. Bennett (captain), G. O. Edwards; G. Price, R. W. Windsor, A. G. Faulkner, A. J. Martin, G. A. D. Wheel, J. Squire, T. J. Cobner, D. L. Quinnell

Referee: G. Domercq (France)

# 8 'Only a Third-Division Side'

## Montluçon 22 Skewen 52, Montluçon, France, 25 September 1972

I take my food seriously – very seriously. My wife Maureen would agree that I have an unhealthy appetite for someone meant to be of diminutive size. Not only do I appreciate good food, but I like the niceties of what Delia Smith might call the preparation of a meal. Now, who can better the French when it comes to arranging gourmet safaris?

I shall never forget the meals – they call them banquets – after matches in France, nor the enormous gastronomic events which Cardiff enjoyed when we visited Cognac. When the cigars are lit, and the belts are slackened, Edwards is in his element. The whiff of garlic or the promise of eleven courses with suitably appropriate wines is an invitation I can never turn down. But for all the enjoyment of the trips to Paris, whether for international matches or representing Cardiff on some of their notable Gallican trips, there was one visit to France which neither I nor the others involved will ever forget.

'Do you remember that weekend when we went to Montluçon?' It's a question that immediately summons a response and a thousand laughs from those on the trip.

My employer, Jack Hamer, had somehow got himself

involved with a group of French Rotarians, who had challenged, or rather asked Jack if he would gather a team to cross the Channel for a special match. Never one to shirk that kind of request and no doubt aided by a vintage of some sort, Jack agreed – and then told me to get on with arranging an Invitation XV. Even as a schoolboy, I used to doodle with pen and paper picking the best Welsh teams, then the best British teams, the best of the Universe and so on. In 1972 I started pencilling in most of the 1971 Lions. On paper I had a magnificent team; I even phoned Pierre Villepreux to be my fullback.

The match was to be played at Montluçon. I have to admit I had not the slightest idea where it was, except that it was somewhere in France. But Jack convinced me that it would be a right royal weekend and that the boys would enjoy themselves, no holds barred. Writing down a team and getting them to come was another matter, however. Most of the players I initially thought of were either tied to their clubs, had to attend weddings or the like, or even had to report for work. I spent a fortune on the telephone and eventually settled on a team consisting largely of Cardiff and Neath players.

Now as luck – or misfortune – would have it, Cardiff were due to play Neath on the afternoon of our departure for Paris. That in itself didn't present any major problems as far as establishing a rendezvous point, but I wondered how some of the invited players would react after the match. Anyone who has witnessed a Cardiff–Neath clash will appreciate my anxiety – and let me add that two of 'my players' were Cardiff's Ian Robinson and Neath's Brian Thomas.

John Spencer, of Headingley, good man that he is, had promised to travel down from Yorkshire to meet us at Heathrow. Arthur Lewis, of Ebbw Vale, had also agreed to come. But there was quite a fuss about Phil Bennett's movements that weekend. He had asked his committee if he might be excused playing for Llanelli that Saturday – Benny is never one to miss a good trip! – which enabled him to travel up to Cardiff and watch the Neath match in our committee box. At the time there had been speculation that my Cardiff club-mate Barry John was contemplating retirement, so the press boys behind the committee box and several spectators were given a lot of food for thought as Phil sat down with the Cardiff committee. Of course, they had no notion of the real reason for the presence of the Wizard from the West.

There was a small problem – when is there never one? – with the Welsh Rugby Union touring regulations. Naturally, we couldn't travel as the Jack Hamer/Gareth Edwards XV, so someone had the bright idea of inviting two representatives of Skewen Rugby Club, their chairman and their scrum half, Johnny Jones. This enabled us to become a bona fide expedition – and Skewen RFC for the next forty-eight hours boasted eight internationals, a handful of Barbarians and six Lions.

The Cardiff–Neath clash meanwhile had lived up to its thunderous tradition – 'Robbo' and 'Twmws' greeted each other at the first scrum, as was their wont, and duly compared bruises over a pint in the bar afterwards. There wasn't time, however, to discuss much in the way of other details of the match. We had barely three hours to get from Cardiff to Heathrow for a flight to France. I reckon I must have come pretty close to the landspeed record as I tore up the M4 with the belly of my overloaded car a centimetre or so from the tarmac. Somehow we all arrived at the airport, breathless but in time to board. Only those who have organized such an outing will fully appreciate the difficulties of keeping tabs on a party of rugby players, keeping them together to travel from A to B and go through all the formalities of booking in, registering luggage and getting aboard the plane. And I thought the hard part was picking the team in the first place!

We had no real idea what kind of opposition faced us. Jack

insisted that this was only a Rotarian trip and we would be playing something like a third-division French club side. Some of us were a trifle sceptical, for we had had experience of similar trips and knew full well that the French had a reputation for stacking their sides with guest players. Every match out there, it seemed, even schoolboy friendlies, was billed as an international, and the French have few superiors when it comes to organizing a little razzmatazz.

'Boys,' Jack said with some assurance, 'you don't have to worry. This is only a friendly, organized by a few pals of mine.' Thus consoled, we arrived in Paris having drunk the plane dry soon after we had crossed the white cliffs of Dover – the stewardess didn't even manage to offer any service to the folk in the front end of the plane. But I must admit that most of what was consumed went to a very merry band of supporters. It was past ten o'clock by the time we reached Paris, our overnight stop, and away we all went for a magnificent meal which was part of the arrangements. The rest of the night, with Robbo and Twmws in the van, was a bit of a blurr. With our departure for Montluçon scheduled for 7.30 next morning, not many of the party had more than a few hours' sleep.

What a sight we turned out to be the next day! The groans, the moans and the agonies of this celebrated team were right out of *MASH*. Jack's 'two to three hour' coach journey to Montluçon turned out to be a five-hour calamity, with everyone twisting and cavorting in their seats in an effort to find the most comfortable position. Half the pack looked green on departure. They were purple on arrival – and we had a match to play!

'Don't worry boys,' Jack said, 'they are only a third-division side.' He then retired to the front of the coach with the tour 'committee', who by now had got their second wind and were enjoying undiluted Scotch as hair of the dog.

Between road diversions and stops of necessity, our ETA at Montluçon was exactly that – estimated. For some of our party a jog around the park had all the appeal of fifteen rounds with Muhammad Ali.

When, at last, we arrived at Montluçon, the locals gave us a tremendous welcome. They had arranged the fixture half expecting that Jack Hamer's team would not make an appearance. (I wonder why?) But welcoming a team from Wales was one thing, seeing a team full of internationals was another. Some of them were a little angry with themselves. 'If only we had known, then the whole area would have been here this afternoon,' they complained, clearly having underestimated Jack's bona fides and the promise of a good weekend. Bells started ringing, bands started playing and those well enough to grip a pen signed their autographs by the hundred.

Naturally, because this was France, an official reception had been laid on. A betting man would have laid long odds on any of the Skewen party looking at an alcoholic drink, let alone imbibing. But down in Neath they've got metal boxes for stomachs, and in a twinkling several bottles of the local vintage were disposed of. Naturally, whatever a Neath man can do, a Cardiff man isn't far behind. . . Some of us could only blink in amazement as Cardiff took up the challenge of the Neath contingent. And we still had a huge meal in front of us. By this time it was my turn, as captain considerate, to seek assurances about the opposition.

Enough to say that some time later we took the field in front of a crowd around 2000, who had already warmed to the occasion by applauding their team, who had run up and down in front of the stand in a gymnastic display intended to prove they were world-beaters. Our pre-kick-off activity was, in comparison, geriatric.

Jack Hamer took up his position in the stand. He sat next

to the mayor. He was veritably beaming as the representatives of Skewen RFC were announced over the public address.

'Wyn Davies, Neath.' (Big cheers.)

'Wayne Lewis, Cardiff and London Welsh.' (More big cheers.)

'Arthur Lewis, Ebbw Vale, Wales, Barbarians and Lions.' (Cheers now deafening.)

And so it went on. By the time the whole team had been announced, the crowd was on its feet, shouting and stamping. What a performance! What a reception!

Although we sounded like a magnificent collection of rugby players, we would have had to bribe a vet to pass us for human exertion. That this glassy-eyed bunch was not seeing very well was confirmed when someone noticed that, despite their introduction, conspicuous by their absence from the field were John Spencer and Arthur Lewis. We found them fast asleep in the changing room.

The first twenty minutes of the match will stay with me for ever. We kicked off, they gathered and before anyone was inclined even to lay a finger on one of the Gallican opposition, they were in a group congratulating themselves on a splendid try. Well, I thought, these things do happen. So I took no real heed – after all I could rely on our forwards. There were four capped players and the bulk of the Cardiff and Neath eights on duty. Montluçon received from the kick-off again – bang! – a dropped goal. Fluke, I assured myself, just wait for the first scrum or line-out. By now, of course, the French side had begun to believe in themselves and their confidence was sky high. The crowd could hardly believe what was happening. Neither could Jack 'They're only a third-division side' Hamer. He was hiding behind the mayor's cloak. Kick-off again – whooosh! – another score to them and we hadn't even touched the ball.

Clearly it was time for the captain to assert himself. I

turned around and spotted Arthur Lewis. 'Come on, Arthur, tackle the blighters,' I pleaded.

'Tackle 'em?' Arthur responded. 'Gar, I can't even see the b—s.'

We were 18 points down after fifteen minutes and I think the mayor was about to declare a public holiday.

Now there is a touch of arrogance about the French when they are dominant. Come to that, the same can be said of the Welsh. But this one bloke in the Montluçon team was giving our boys a bit of a caning in the rucks and mauls. Friendly or no friendly, Twmws doesn't like being messed about. So at the next scrum he inquired politely of Glyn Shaw as to the Neath prop's willingness to deal with the French skirmisher. Glyn accepted Twmws's reasoning and duly obliged. The troublemaker took no further part in the affair.

Glyn's intervention may have proved the turning point for within minutes Tommy 'Me, myself, personally' David scored one of those tries in which he did a fair impersonation of dragging a coal train from Cilfynydd to Cardiff, Frenchmen loaded on his shoulders by the ton. Suddenly, Skewen began to assume their responsibilities. There was a match to be won.

After half time it was unbelievable rugby. Whatever we tried came off. Passes went to hand, reverse scissors were timed to perfection, and so masterly was our control of the mid-field that by the end we even tried to contrive a try for Roger Beard.

Eventually we won by 52–22, Jack Hamer reappeared from behind the mayor's cloak and it was time to rejoin the wine tasting. The carnival atmosphere at Montluçon continued through the night, from the after-match reception to night clubs, from toast to toast. The open generosity of the townsfolk was incredible. We drank, ate and laughed until the early hours, when Jack, timing his moment nicely announced, 'I told you, didn't I. They were only a third-division side.'

The funniest moment of the trip concerned Arthur Lewis. Suddenly, whilst eating, Arthur leaped to his feet, his face puce. We could make nothing of his grunts and snorts as he gesticulated and pointed to his mouth. Mervyn John was convinced that he was merely making a grandiose attempt to obtain more wine. He offered the spluttering Arthur a bottle. Only later, in the toilet, when the offending chicken bone was removed from Arthur's throat, did we realize how close we had come to losing a member of the tour party.

Skewen: Wyn Davies (Neath); Wayne Lewis (London Welsh, Cardiff), Arthur Lewis (Ebbw Vale), John Spencer (Headingley), Ian Hall (Aberavon); Phil Bennett (Llanelli), Gareth Edwards (Cardiff) (captain); Roger Beard (Cardiff), Gary Davies (Cardiff), Glyn Shaw (Neath), Brian Thomas (Neath), Ian Robinson (Cardiff), Mervyn Davies (Cardiff), Tommy David (Pontypridd/Llanelli), Barry Davies (Neath)

# 9 Hamstrings

Without fear of contradiction, I think my hamstrings are famous in the wide world of rugby. I have been accused of having hamstring mania, of inventing hamstring complaints which do not exist in the medical textbooks, and of using them as an excuse for not playing in certain club matches.

'Those hamstrings of yours are all in your head' – so spake, often, Dr Doug Smith, manager of the 1971 Lions team in New Zealand. He also suggested that they belonged to another part of my anatomy, but I won't go into that. All I can say is that the athlete who has never suffered from a pull will never know the psychological trauma caused by that sudden, sharp pain which cripples and is followed by long periods when one's confidence to run is completely undermined.

Most people, including some of the medical fraternity, say a hamstring pull is the result of failing to warm up properly before physical exercise. That can't be true, because I've suffered at the fag end of a match and also when I've been at peak fitness. Invariably, hamstrings suffer when the body has been asked to do something immediate and explosive. The worst aspect is not knowing when the next one will come, and not having enough faith in your legs to respond to the challenge at hand. On a few occasions, I admit, I have nursed myself along, fully aware that if I had adopted my natural game. I would inevitably end the match on the physio's couch.

No one knows more about the 'Edwards's hamstrings' than the former Welsh trainer, Gerry Lewis. Gerry is a remarkable man. I gave him a clock before my fiftieth cap, to thank him for making it possible for me to have attained that number of appearances. Without his diligent attention I'm sure I wouldn't have played a quarter of the matches at scrum half for Wales.

Another thing about hamstrings. They give you the power of total recall!

I remember, back in 1977, a match between Cardiff and Llanelli in the Welsh Cup. Hefin Jenkins, the Llanelli back-row forward landed on my back and I knew immediately something was wrong. The pain was so excruciating I had to go off. Wales were due to play Ireland the following Saturday and the chances of winning my No. 48 cap seemed remote. I sought opinion after opinion throughout the week prior to the Irish match and it became increasingly likely that my consecutive run of appearances for Wales would have to come to an end. Then someone suggested it wasn't my hamstring at all, but a back injury. Gordon Rowley, the WRU medical officer, agreed – suddenly the world seemed a better place.

I confess now that the doubts about the hamstring prevailed and I admit that I coasted against the Irish, concentrating on kicking for territorial gain instead of probing for openings. It was very frustrating, for often I saw some mighty gaps in the Irish defence.

Understandably, I received a roasting from the press with the north stand typewriters machine-gunning out the criticism: 'subdued', 'off-colour' or 'below par'. I suppose, on reflection, it could have been worse. They might have suggested I should be dropped! Yet only forty-eight hours earlier I had told the Welsh selectors that I wouldn't be able to play. Ironically, my own performance did not merit the headlines. Those were taken up by the dual sending off of Geoff Wheel and Willie Duggan.

There were other times when I feared that the legs wouldn't hold out. In the circumstances, I had to tell friends and the media a few white lies.

I remember coming off the field during a Welsh training session at Bridgend in considerable pain. Those with imminent deadlines hurried over to me to inquire of my health. 'Nothing serious, boys,' I told them, 'just a blister.' How I kept a straight and honest countenance I do not know. I was in agony and could barely move. Gerry Lewis, good old Gerry, got to work on my fibres over the next two days, and it was that treatment which enabled me to take the field and play against Australia.

Why the hamstring trouble started. I'm not quite sure. It is possible that my early days as a high hurdler at Millfield didn't help, but the complaint proper began during the Lions training at Eastbourne preparatory to the tour of South Africa in 1968. It flared up again during the Welsh tour of New Zealand in 1969 and, most exasperatingly, before the First Test against the All Blacks during the 1971 Lions tour. No matter how much treatment I received – in fact I underwent a manipulative operation in 1973 – the problem stayed with me throughout my career. Some have even suggested that I played one match for Cardiff against Llanelli with two hamstring pulls!

If there was one 'hamstring match' which stood out, it was Wales against South Africa in 1970.

## Wales 6 South Africa 6, Cardiff Arms Park, 24 January 1970

As I am often reminded, Wales have never beaten South Africa, home or away. When the Springboks toured Britain in 1970, we felt at the time that we had a better than even chance of removing the one blot on the Welsh copybook.

That tour was highlighted by student demonstrations and riots, and it attracted considerable controversy, with anti-apartheid protesters hounding the South Africans wherever they went. The tourists were shepherded from one hotel to another in great secrecy, making life extremely difficult for the players. The off-the-field activities impinged on most of those who played against the South Africans. When I played against them, for Cardiff, I had the distinct impression that they were trying to disguise their real feelings and that their play was being affected. There was a huge demonstration at Swansea, but generally the Springboks had a relatively placid time in the Welsh part of the tour.

In those days Wales still staged trials, and although we had been given a caning in New Zealand the previous summer there was evidence that a transformation in our fortunes was under way. There were a number of young players coming through, and some of the older 'generals' of the late sixties were now content to take their place in the former internationals section in the south stand at the Arms Park. Wales was to be the last home country to do battle against the Springboks, who had beaten England and Scotland, and, on the day of our final Welsh trial, had drawn with Ireland. The tourists desperately wanted to wind up a generally frustrating tour with a victory – and a win at the Arms Park would suit the bill just fine.

In the trial – disaster! That old familiar jab in the back of the thigh, the consequent emotional shock, and the Springboks to be met in a fortnight's time. It may not have been a bad pull, certainly not the worst. Yet it required several daily visits to Gerry Lewis.

Match day against the Springboks turned out to be the worst hamstring weather of all. It had rained, it seemed, for forty days and forty nights on Cardiff, and the Arms Park, constantly in use those days, was generally the worst of any international ground. Although it had the advantage of being right in the centre of the city, often it was like walking out to play on a construction site. I didn't feel sorry for the South Africans having to play on this mud heap – a cloudburst on match day had turned the pitch into a bog – but I could imagine their thoughts, particularly as they had been reared on bone-hard pitches back in South Africa.

The demonstrators were there in numbers as well; so were the obligatory officers of the law. Sometimes I would smile at the number of duty policemen at the Arms Park, all of them getting a splendid view, but on this day they could hardly have relished attending to the demonstrators as the heavens opened.

But I had my own share of problems. In the mud perhaps the leg would not hold out, particularly as it was certain that the game would require many a thrust from the base of the scrum. No one in his right mind could have expected an attractive match, or an open one. It was going to be a battle between the packs and the halfbacks. And I did not need reminding that Ellis, Bedford and Greyling, the pre-eminent South African back row, would be eager and willing to exploit any weaknesses on the part of the Welsh scrum half!

It poured and poured, and life was most unpleasant. The barbed wire surrounding the field added to the unreality of the match. Wales, it must be said, were a bit inclined to play a dry-weather game at the beginning, and the Springboks improved their play as the match progressed.

Henry de Villiers put them ahead with a penalty goal in the first half when we were caught off side at a line-out, a sector of play in which we were struggling to gain parity. They might also have scored a try before half time, but the temptation to kick in the conditions proved too much for Roux and, fortunately for Wales, Nomis was denied a potential try. In those conditions a try at that stage probably would have sealed the result. In the event, Wales were awarded a penalty, which I kicked. That was a touch arrogant considering I had Barry John and Phil Bennett in the side.

There was little respite in the second half, and before we had properly settled down Nomis made up for his first-half disappointment by scoring a try in the corner following a pass by Lawless, the Springbok fly half.

Throughout the match I was conscious of the strain on my leg and I was crossing my fingers that it wouldn't give in on me. I focused on gathering the ball cleanly which, because of the slippery conditions, always seemed to land in that vacant area between forwards and scrum half – a no-go area if you had a mind to stay healthy.

After their try, the South Africans were that much more determined. Probably they felt that the lead was sufficient to see them through. I also felt that tactically they were superior to us. The minutes ticked away to no-side and most of the Welsh team were conceding the possibility that we were booked for yet another defeat at the hands of the Springboks. Larry Lamb, the referee, had already checked his watch and a good number of rain-soaked spectators were making their way to the exits.

Then it happened. No, not a hamstring pull. That psychological torment was to come. Phil Bennett, out on the wing, threw a long infield pass to Barry, who kicked for the corner. Ian Hall homed in on Nomis and, aided by John Dawes, held the South African wing long enough for Barry Llewelyn to race up and prise the ball loose. It may seem inconceivable, but I can remember every stride as I tore up to take Barry's flipped pass. My frantic, initial thoughts were of protecting my hamstring, but they immediately dissolved as I gathered full pace. Had I started from a stationary position, a run for the line in the mud would have been foolhardy. As it was, I had the ball and was really moving. It helped too that the South African back row had been drawn into the maul that had formed around Norris. There are moments when the action freezes, or seems to, and you have time to analyse the best course of action. Sometimes the gaps appear to be as big as the Arms Park gates. You have to take these opportunities whenever they occur, because gaps close just as rapidly as they appear. So when Barrie gave me the ball, I surged for the line. There were about 25 metres between me and score, and I suddenly started thinking again about that hamstring. Will it hold out, or will I be caught just before the line? The mental torture had begun.

The first few strides were fine and suddenly I was really motoring. I could see the policemen at the other end and I was conscious of making the corner flag my target. More for my leg, than anything, I uttered a little prayer. Ten metres to go and I knew, hamstring or no hamstring, I simply had to make it. If it had gone there and then, I would have felt such a fool, and the mud, the darned mud was still cloying, trying to cut my pace and impetus. Three metres left – and still no twinge. At last, I knew I was going to make it. I slithered in and the crowd went wild. We were level, but my elation was a personal one, entirely of relief that for one of the most important runs of my life the leg had held out. I danced around like a footballer who has just scored the winning goal in the Cup Final. Some might have thought my reaction, spontaneous though it was, smacked of immaturity. Rugby players just do not do *that* sort of thing! I couldn't have cared less. In fact I felt so good, so pleased with myself that I automatically took the ball out to the touchline for the conversion, a kick that I knew would win Wales their first victory ever over the Springboks. J.P.R. came up and offered to take the kick and, of course, I had Phil and Barry to call on. The South Africans meanwhile were distraught, standing forlornly in the rain behind their posts waiting for a kick that, quite undeservedly, would spell defeat for them. I refused J.P.R's offer and prepared to take the kick myself. History will show that I missed it. And although I may never be charged with treasonable thoughts, in a way I was somewhat relieved when the kick didn't go over. Wales didn't deserve to win and South Africa didn't deserve to lose. Even a draw did not reflect their overall superiority; as players, they deserved a lot of sympathy for enduring all the off-the-field problems. Wales were damned lucky, and I trotted off to seek out Gerry Lewis and his slab.

Wales: J. P. R. Williams; P. Bennett, S. J. Dawes, W. H. Raybould, I. Hall; B. John, G. O. Edwards (captain); D. Williams, V. C. Perrins, D. B. Llewelyn, W. D. Thomas, T. G. Evans, W. D. Morris, D. Hughes, T. M. Davies

South Africa: H. O. de Villiers; S. H. Nomis, Q. A. Roux, J. P. van der Merwe, G. H. Muller; M. J. Lawless, D. J. de Villiers (captain); J. L. Myburgh, C. H. Cockrell, J. F. K. Marais, F. C. H. du Preez, I. J. de Klerk, P. J. F. Greyling, J. H. Ellis, T. P. Bedford

Referee: G. C. Lamb (England)

# 10 Wales *versus* France

Oysters, lobsters, rare beef, wine and cognac – how I love the French! I started and finished my international career against them, and I hold them above all other teams as the most dangerous and formidable opponents.

They are never to be underestimated, even when they are behind, and they can dazzle the opposition when they have a commanding lead. Perhaps it is their instinctive ability to adopt the dangerous ploy that has impressed me – back-row moves from defence, magnetic handling by every man on the field, and their zest to keep the momentum of a movement going. A lapse of concentration against the French, no matter how brief, can give them the impetus they need, because they are the masters of innovation and capitalization.

My first cap, at Stade Colombes, and the experiences of Welsh international baptism would provide good copy for a sit-com script. A friend had to double-check whether I had been selected in the first place – at my insistence, of course. Another turned up in my hotel room on the morning of the match, his clothes flavoured with Gallican ingredients. And my brief safari into a Paris shopping precinct for fishing tackle – yes, even in those days – nearly had the Welsh XV scrum half posted as missing. It all happened so quickly, and the excitable, nervous, uninhibited passion of a nineteen-year-old made time fly. It was nothing like the calm, detached approach I adopted in my final match against France in Cardiff.

During the seventies the Welsh XV had, through familiarity and coaching, become such a formidable piece of machinery that we could take the field knowing that the ability was there to overcome all obstacles. It may be arrogant to suggest that in 1978, when France had gone into a 7–0 lead, I knew that something or someone on our side would turn events to our advantage. The man who did it was Phil Bennett, with two tries. What a way to end his career – becoming the first Welsh fly half since Raymond Ralph (also against France, at St Helen's, Swansea, in 1931) to score a brace of tries. Phil was aided and abetted by two dropped goals, another rare event for a Welsh team, from yours truly and Steve Fenwick. Steve's dropped goal was one of the most opportunistic – and ugly – ever executed at the Arms Park, at least in comparison to the modest little effort from the Welsh scrum half! It was, of course, another example of the depth of talent of that Welsh side, which could call upon a vast range of weaponry to defeat the opposition to make some matches a comforting and comfortable experience.

## France 20 Wales 14, Stade Colombes, Paris, 1 April 1967

My introduction to international rugby and my preparation for my first match for Wales was, to say the least, haphazard. After Wales had lost to Ireland by a try to nothing at the Arms Park, the selectors disposed of Grahame Hodgson, Ken Braddock, Alun Pask and Allan Lewis. Pask, in fact, had withdrawn because of the death of his brother, but he was never picked for Wales again. I was one of three new caps, for into a reshaped back row came Ron Jones and Dai Morris.

I replaced Allan Lewis to partner Dai Watkins, who was captaining Wales for the second time. Dai was one of the mainstays of the Welsh side at the time, for only Dewi Bebb and Brian Price had made more championship match appearances.

Such reshuffling in mid-season meant that some of the newcomers were just that. We had not only not played with some of the established stars, but, as in my case with Dai Watkins, we were relative strangers, having only met for the first time and played together in a trial the previous December. Our second meeting actually took place at the Arms Park a few nights before our departure for Paris. It speaks volumes for our 'fame' that we had to convince Cardiff officials that we really were the Welsh halfbacks before they grudgingly consented to let us have the use of a ball to rehearse a few moves. Even then, it must have been an odd sight. Neither Dai nor I had changed from our street clothes and there we were, two solitary figures in suits on a deserted Arms Park, getting to know each other with a ball we were lucky to have borrowed. To think that in a few days' time we had to face France in Paris in an important championship match – not the meat to ruffle the feathers of the French Cockerel.

The rest of the week, the trip over to Paris, the sightseeing, the ritual of preparing for the match in the changing room – all rushed past in a long, continuous blurr. Suddenly my debut for Wales was over almost before I had realized that it had happened.

Incidents in the match, however, were in sharp relief. I remember concentrating like mad on getting the ball quickly and accurately to Dai Watkins. Then there was my baptism of another sort – a stiff-arm tackle from Benoît Dauga, the French No. 8. I recall too Dewi Bebb dribbling an enormous distance for Wales's only try, and Terry Price, in his final appearance for Wales, missing six out of nine kicks at goal.

The most singularly distinct memory, however, was of the dapper figure of Guy Cambérabéro destroying us almost on his own with 14 of France's 20 points – two dropped goals, a try, a conversion and a penalty. I also remember with anguish that Cambérabéro missed one penalty kick – only for the ball to rebound from a post into play and for Claude Dourthe to pick up and score a try. Cambérabéro rubbed salt into the wound by converting it.

That was France's fifth win in a row against Wales in Paris, and remains their best winning sequence against us. What a day to make one's debut! There were, however, consolations in defeat: I had experienced the pace and pressure of playing in France and I received lasting mementoes of the occasion in the shape of the match ball, courtesy of Dewi Bebb, and a French jersey, courtesy of Christian Darrouy, the French captain. The remainder of the trip seems to be a rapid sequence of disjointed scenes, fused together by one reality – I had won my first cap for Wales. Somewhere in the nether regions of the mind, there was the important personal warmth of family support, the bewilderment and agony of the match banquet, at which I was entranced by the amount of cutlery set out before us. There was too the obligatory late-night junketing at Montmartre and other dubious haunts under the auspices of two worldly-wise Welsh selectors, who gave me the distinct impression that they had been there before. But that is another story.

France: J. Gachassin; M. Arnaudet, C. Dourthe, J.-P. Lux, C. Darrouy (captain); G. Cambérabéro, L. Cambérabéro; A. Gruarin, J.-M. Cabanier, J.-C. Berejnoi, E. Cester, J. Fort, M. Sitjar, C. Carrère, B. Dauga

Wales: T. G. Price; S. J. Watkins, W. H. Raybould, T. G. R. Davies, D. I. E. Bebb; D. Watkins (captain), G. O. Edwards; D. Williams, B. I. Rees, D. J. Lloyd, B. Price, M. T. Mainwaring, R. E. Jones, J. Taylor, W. D. Morris

Referee: D. P. d'Arcy (Ireland)

## France 5 Wales 9, Stade Colombes, Paris, 27 March 1971

As I have already intimated, the 1971 Welsh side was the best to represent Wales during my international career. It had been tested and emerged with growing credit from matches against England, Scotland and Ireland, and the final examination was in Paris in the springtime. The French welcome was warm as usual – on and off the field!

The French do not need much in the way of encouragement to perform well against Wales. It almost seems inherent. It is enough to say they thundered around Stade Colombes like men possessed, and even Barry John was required to put in a tackle or two! The Grand Slam, that precious, most elusive of the Five Nations Championship 'trophies', awaited us if we could conquer the French. But they were not about to let us take the prize without some show of resistance. Resistance *myn uffern i*! We were nearly run off our feet in the first half, when the French, with the wind, were devastating. Obviously we were going to need if not divine intervention, at least Lady Fortune to smile on us. She did. The French were threatening close to our line when J.P.R. with masterful judgement, intercepted a Roger Bourgarel pass, to race out of the danger area. (Bourgarel might well have gibbed at that moment and thrown a desperate pass, for earlier J.P.R. had almost cut him in half with a tackle.) But what a distance faced J.P.R., what a run he had to make! Fair play to Denzil Williams, that mighty man from Ebbw Vale – he decided to partner John part of the way, though I'm sure the doctor would have preferred swifter company. There is nothing I like more than the unexpected move. So I travelled past the tiring Denzil and, aligning myself outside J.P.R., I shouted, 'Japes, here!' and took his pass to score in the corner. I didn't really expect to score, I didn't think I'd make the line. It was poaching, pure and simple, I must be honest. At the time we didn't deserve that score and we were lucky to get it. But that's rugby. One moment you are down and almost out. The next, the situation and the match have changed completely. Later on, Barry John performed a piece of his own special brand of magic, sliding through a French door that was only partly ajar. That, plus a penalty, were the only Welsh scores on a torrid afternoon, but they proved sufficient to gain us a victory that the critics by and large hailed. It could have been more had Barry and J.P.R. succeeded with a few more kicks. But that would hardly have been justice to a French side who played their hearts out. Certainly they played to their supporters. The stadium throbbed with emotion, the French fans willing their side on and the fewer Welsh supporters praying that we could end a nineteen-year wait for the Grand Slam.

Although that 1971 side was branded as slow starters, there was an undeniable collective will to win. I cannot remember one moment of frustration because someone did not do his job or pull his weight. From J.P.R. down to Barry Llewelyn, the team had quality in strength, talent behind and one of the most effective back rows ever.

It was not surprising that most of that side were soon on a plane bound for the great adventure, the Lions tour of New Zealand which turned out to be so successful. The only surprise was in the players who did not go.

France: P. Villepreux; R. Bourgarel, R. Bertranne, J.-P. Lux, J. Cantoni; J.-L. Bérot, M. Barrau; J. Iraçabal, R. Bénésis, M. Lasserre, C. Spanghéro, W. Spanghéro, B. Dauga, J.-P. Biemouret, C. Carrère (captain)

Wales: J. P. R. Williams; T. G. R. Davies, S. J. Dawes (captain), A. J. Lewis, J. C. Bevan; B. John, G. O. Edwards; D. B. Llewelyn, J. Young, D. Williams, W. D. Thomas, M. G. Roberts, W. D. Morris, J. Taylor, T. M. Davies

Referee: J. Young (Scotland)

## Wales 16 France 7, Cardiff Arms Park, 18 March 1978

My last appearance in a Welsh jersey coincided with the departure from the championship scene of Phil Bennett, Terry Cobner, Gareth Evans, Jean-Claude Skréla and Jean-Pierre Bastiat, each of whom in his own way had made a valuable contribution to rugby in Wales and France. It seemed appropriate that we should all sign off, as it were, in a match in which the Grand Slam was the prize for the side that won.

Unlike some of the others, however, I had made my own conscious decision to retire. This explains, I suppose, the curious feeling of detachment from the usual razzmatazz of an international morning in Cardiff. True, Westgate Street was a blaze of colour, newspaper placards, touts, friends waiting for friends who were an hour late, people with microphones asking the same questions in a different order, and the Angel Hotel creating another record jam. But this time I resisted the temptation of total immersion.

The business of a match morning always stiffens the resolve and quickens the blood, but this day possessed a certain tranquillity. The walk from the hotel room down the corridor was always a lonely one. Television pictures on 'Grandstand' and the ritualistic preparations kept you in touch with the goings-on in and around the ground. But that hotel corridor was a haven which allowed one time to think, to suspend emotion for precious, brief moments, and to come to terms with what had to be done in the afternoon. I always kept thinking on the way to the ground how I would feel on the return journey.

On this final journey from the hotel to the Arms Park I resolved to take in everything and commit all experiences to memory. After all, it was going to be the last time I did it. Before a match I always liked to throw a pass. It didn't particularly matter who the recipient was, but at least it was something constructive to do. Most of the boys just run out onto the pitch in a frenzied manner not knowing what to do next. Some bend their knees, others sprint to the corners, each one in a world of his own, fraught, tense and anxious to get on with the matter in hand. The international rugby player at that moment is so psyched up that he is barely aware of the crowd, the anthems or any other distraction. Yet on this day, my last match for Wales, I looked around, spotted my parents in their seats, watched the crowd and took it all in.

It hadn't been difficult to motivate myself for the farewell appearance. The newly emerging French scrum half, Jérôme Gallion, had been highly praised for his performance against Ireland, and countless newspaper columns had been devoted to the battle between the 'ageing' master and this gifted young pupil. I didn't mind that, because more than anything it sharpened the senses. Towards the end of my career, I suppose the predictability of the pre-match expectation had dulled the acute excitement I once felt. The anticipation of the challenge from the talented youngster from Stade Toulouse was enough to bring me into line again. I knew what I enjoyed most at that stage was being part of a disciplined orchestra, and there was no greater satisfaction than picking up the baton and leading the charges against the opposition.

The French, with Gallion in good form, and the devastating energy of Skréla and Jean-Pierre Rives, had us reeling in the opening twenty minutes. I still felt that the composure of the Welsh team would see us through. As in 1971, there were so many match-winners behind the scrum. It was merely a question of time, of containing the early French ferocity and then taking control. The forwards gave me sufficient ball to expose the flanks with long kicks – there is nothing which causes more disharmony among the enemy ranks than being pushed back over hard-fought-for ground by such kicking. A ground-consuming kick also has the bonus of perking up your own team. So it was against France, my first international opponents and now, fittingly, my last. Bastiat stalked the line-outs like a hungry giraffe and we had to live off the crumbs. But the Welsh team had been nurtured by success after success. The ingredient called confidence brought stability of thought and action. And there were J.P.R., J.J., Steve Fenwick and Benny to provide the unorthodox touches, those bolts from the blue that shattered the opposition.

Two factors gave me immense pleasure that afternoon. One was Gallion who, unknown to him, had perked up my performance, and the other was the fact that he came up to me at the end of the match and, in a humble, almost deprecating manner, thanked me. Why Gallion did that, I do not know. But this was another gesture of friendship which has endeared me to the French over the years.

What spurred my decision to retire? There had been no pressure from family or friends. Perhaps it was the Welsh fan who had said, 'Off to Australia now, back for the All Blacks in September, and then a Lions tour?' which threw up the possibility, the notion and then the inevitability.

It had been a magnificent season. The England match at Twickenham had provided me with my fiftieth appearance for Wales, there was the Triple Crown to savour, and now finally the Grand Slam. The end had to come some time, and why not with the finale to a great season for Welsh rugby.

I did not want to go out of the game having outstayed my welcome. I had no desire to play another decade, ending up in wooden changing huts on freezing Saturday afternoons. When a few of my friends said that I was playing as well as ever, I knew at once that it was time to go; they might not have been so generous had I stayed for another term of office in the No. 9 jersey. And there were other forces, apart from commercial ones, which had more or less determined that this was to be my last match.

That is why I remained as detached as possible, not wanting the day or its experiences to end. Of course, it had been so different from my first appearance. Then, faithfully, as he had always done, my father had cleaned my boots; my mother had made sure I possessed clean socks, shirt and pants; my brother-in-law gave me a dinner jacket. And yet no sooner had I emerged from the strange tunnel at Stade Colombes than I seemed to be trudging wearily back down it. The first and last matches – emotional peaks. Time does not erase their memories.

Oh, I almost forgot, Wales beat France – eventually – and took the Grand Slam. Thanks to Benny and his two tries and a couple of dropped goals.

Wales: J. P. R. Williams; J. J. Williams, R. W. R. Gravell, S. P. Fenwick, G. L. Evans; P. Bennett (captain), G. O. Edwards; G. Price, R. W. Windsor, A. G. Faulkner, A. J.

Martin, G. A. D. Wheel, J. Squire, T. J. Cobner, D. L. Quinnell

France: J.-M. Aguirre; D. Bustaffa, R. Bertranne, C. Belascain, G. Novès. B. Viviès, J. Gallion; R. Paparemborde, A. Paco, G. Cholley, F. Haget, M. Palmié, J.-C. Skréla, J.-P. Rives, J.-P. Bastiat (captain)

Referee: A. Welsby (England)